Just a Phone Call Away

JUST A
PHONE CALL
AWAY

Scotti Madison

Aaron —
Work Hard and don't let
anyone still your dreams —
Hope you enjoy —
My Best —
Scotti Madison

Contents

Acknowledgments

There are certainly many friends and family members to thank in my fifty-four years for loving me and supporting me spiritually and emotionally during the dark days. The need to recognize these friends and family is just as important when it comes to the reality of writing this book. Yet there are so many of you whom I consider friends and so many family members that I love, that I believe I could write an entire book just naming you. If your name is not on these pages, do not think for a moment you have not been important to me, for I get my strength through God and through the friends and family he has woven throughout my walk on earth.

To Ronnie Huff, Steve Steinhauer, William Wardlaw, and Tommy Disco, thank you for being there any day I pick up the phone and for being brutally honest with me even when it hurts. Your strength is in your good hearts.

To David Cloud, Jeff Estep, Frank Tamplin, and Tom Giddens, on every call we pick up right where we left off; your friendship is important to me, and I value your loyalty.

To Ray Melvin, Terry Nelson, and Shane Williamson, the times we meet are always uplifting, and I know you pray for me often.

To John Ingram, I appreciate your friendship all the way back to Vanderbilt. Without your guidance, this book would not have happened.

To my father, I know that you have gone the way of the world, but I thank you for playing ball with me every time I asked. I look forward to playing catch with you on the baseball fields in heaven.

To Mom, Ann, Mike, and Miles, we have shed tears of sorrow and laughed until tears filled our eyes with joy; I could not have handpicked a better family.

To Uncle Carl, thank you for teaching me the importance of

hard work. I learned that perfect practice makes the games much more enjoyable.

To Libby, thank you for the years we had.

To Tori and Trent, the apples of my eye, you will always be my favorite daughter and son, and I only hope you recognize just how much I have loved you. I regret you never saw me practice.

To Dimples Kellogg, from day one I liked you and knew you were the perfect editor for me; there is none more enjoyable to work with, and I knew you were good when I heard your name for the first time. "Dimples Kellogg" sounds like an editor.

To Heather, you have brought me so much joy and inspired me to be a better man, a better person, and the man God intended for me to be. It was you who said, "Start writing," and your belief in me helped me type the first word on this journey. You are my best friend.

To my Heavenly Father, if you had blessed me to be a Hall of Fame player, I would have missed out on your mercy and love, and I would have never experienced baseball like I did. Thank you for the trials you put me through. They have allowed me to write.

Introduction

I t was the top of the ninth inning, and the visiting team, the Omaha Royals, was down three runs to the Tidewater Mets the first week of June in 1988. I knew all eyes were on me as I stepped into the batter's box as a pinch hitter to lead off the inning. I had just arrived that day to meet the Omaha Royals on the road in Norfolk, Virginia, a Monday night game at the front end of a three-game series. I was not in the best of moods when I arrived at the yard. After all, my confidence had dwindled to the point of dejection. The customary seventy-two hours that the Major League allows a player who is demoted to the Minor Leagues had just expired. It would take me seventy-one and a half hours to decide during the transition if I even wanted to play baseball anymore.

Recently, my big league manager John Wathan demoted me from the parent club, the Kansas City Royals, and my childhood dreams were shattered. The game of baseball had lessened in importance to me over the past three days, and I was feeling as if I had been fired from a job and experienced a family death in the same moment.

It had been almost a week since my last plate appearance in Kansas City, and even though I was in a depressed state of mind while putting on my unspoiled Triple A uniform for the first time, the instincts of survival soon took hold of me when I entered the batter's box. Adrenaline was now pumping through my well-conditioned body as I glanced at my adversary on the pitching mound. I felt as if I just strode into the Roman Colosseum to participate as a gladiator in a reenactment of a famous battle scene of ancient times.

Once my bat touched home plate, my pride kicked in, and I relied on my trained reflexes not to let me down in my battle for survival. Yes, I was on a new team with new players to impress, but most of all, I needed to impress myself. I desperately needed to believe one more time that I still had what it took to play in the Major Leagues.

I told myself, *It has been a couple of days since you last hit, so let's just take a pitch to see exactly how hard this guy can throw. Be patient, and let's get some timing on this ninety-mile-per-hour fastball.* Quickly, the tall right-hander for the opposition was ahead in the count 0–1 as I contemplated the next offering. Digging my left foot in the batter's box, I guessed that a curveball would be thrown next as the pitch of choice. I kept saying to myself, *Just stay back, wait, see it, and hit it.*

Mike Tyson could have not dropped me any faster to the ground. I was sprawled out, unconscious, across home plate. Tim Darnell Drummond, my six-foot three-inch counterpart, never threw a curveball. I am not even sure what pitch left his right hand, but it felt like a two-pound ball-peen hammer slamming the side of my head.

Eventually, a doctor had to use two dozen stitches to close the gash that only cork, yarn, and horsehide leather could make. The moisture on my face was a combination of summer sweat and blood, but mostly blood. The ball struck me somewhere in the corner of my right eye, the one closest to my view of the pitcher.

Slowly coming to my senses from the errant throw, I recognized Royals trainer Nick Swartz, who asked, "Scotti, are you okay? Do you know where you are?"

I despondently replied, "Nick, I know I'm not in the Major Leagues anymore!"

While lying there dazed and speechless, I saw my entire baseball career flash before my eyes. Now many years and dozens of stitches later, I have decided to share some of those experiences with you, both the good and the bad. There won't be any All-Star appearances and certainly no World Series game to speak of in this story. In fact, there might not even be a baseball card worth collecting.

I never made any money playing baseball, and I will not be

mentioned in the same breath with the great players in the Minor Leagues who were my teammates: Sid Bream, John Franco, Gary Gaetti, Kent Hrbek, Orel Hershiser, and Jeff Reed, to name a few. But when I proudly left America's pastime, I left with all my effort still on the field, and I left with friends. There was nothing I valued more! There was plenty of living from Single A ball to the Major Leagues, always for better or worse, for richer or poorer, until one day I took off my uniform for the last time.

Chapter 1
Dr. Miller High Life

I t seemed like just yesterday, yet it was five years earlier when a doctor in El Paso, Texas, autographed the other side of my face with twenty-one stitches. The day before I experienced my first demotion, mostly at my request, to be sent back to Double A San Antonio, leaving the Albuquerque Dukes. I would meet the San Antonio Dodgers on the road and start catching immediately behind the plate for Manager Terry Collins.

The game with the hometown Diablos was just three innings old when Billy Max, all six feet two inches, 220 pounds of him, decided to freight train me at home plate as he attempted to score from second base. As Billy rounded third base, I was anticipating when the ball would arrive from left field. I could see Billy and the ball in one view, and a "bang, bang" play at the plate seemed inevitable.

This collision, too, was ugly, just like the waylay in Norfolk, Virginia, from a pitched baseball. The train wreck at home plate left gashes in my upper cheek, which were the results of the front edge of Max's helmet slicing it in two places.

The umpire hollered an exuberant, "You're out!" which prompted me to jubilantly spike the ball on top of home plate.

Immediately, the vision in my left eye became a blur while blood rushing from the cuts found the shortest route to the ground. Charlie Strasser, the former trainer, equipment manager, and part-time bullpen catcher, escorted me across the field to the home team dugout. I kept telling Charlie, "Home plate is mine. That was awesome!"

Blood wildly spewed from my left eye while Charlie ushered me down the runway and into the El Paso locker room. The first mirror I came to revealed that I was sliced in two places, above the left eye in the eyebrow line and just below the eye. A razor couldn't have done a better job of it. My first thought was, *I won't be going out with the boys to Juarez on this trip, but I will play tomorrow!*

With blood drenching the top of my Dodgers uniform, I was ready to take the trip to the emergency room, a familiar route in my sports-related past. Moments later, however, a police officer entered the locker room escorting a heavy-set bearded man carrying a brown leather medical bag in one hand and a jumbo cup of beer in the other.

Upon viewing the man's casual appearance and borderline slouch, I wondered, *Is this guy really a doctor?* The strong smell of beer on his breath hit me as the man hovered over my face to assess the damage.

Concerned for my appearance, I asked, "Charlie, what's the deal? We're going to the hospital, aren't we?"

His reply wasn't reassuring: "No! Just relax. Everything is fine! The bearded guy is a doctor I met before the game."

Then he calmly said to the man: "I didn't catch your name, Doc."

I turned to the doctor and asked him how many beers he had consumed thus far. As he reached into his brown leather bag of goodies, he assured me he was sipping on "only" his third of the game.

"Oh, great, one an inning!" I nervously said as the witch doctor exercised his talent one stitch at a time in my left eye while leaning across the right side of my face. I could catch every beer fume from that position.

A plastic surgeon in Vanderbilt's ER could not have done much better at placing sutures. The only major problem facing the operating team of one was the lack of adequate light in the makeshift operating room. The problem was quickly remedied when the police officer volunteered to hold his flashlight over the area of concern in order to ensure proper illumination for Dr. Miller High Life.

A sarcastic thought flashed through my mind: *That is such a thoughtful gesture from the nice officer, since there are only ten stitches to go.*

I managed to make it out of the locker room by the seventh inning stretch, just in time for the good doctor to get one more beer before the concession stands shut down. Unfortunately, this wasn't hockey, so I couldn't return to the game. But I managed to talk Terry Collins into starting me the next night at catcher, even though I had a black eye with all those stitches outlining the dark purple shade spread across the left side of my face. I threatened to go home if I didn't play, even if it was with only one good eye.

It seemed that every time I hit a wall in baseball, and this was one, my memory traveled to the good fortune of my friend and former teammate Kent Hrbek, fondly known as Herbie. It was a pleasant thought, always bringing me comfort and encouragement to carry me onward during the worst of baseball times. My memory went back to Monday, August 24, 1981, when Herbie made his Major League debut with a memorable splash in, of all places, old historic Yankee Stadium, the most famous sports park in the world. Kent not only got his first hit but also soon went down in history as one of those storybook players who hits a home run on his first day in the lineup, the same day that he traversed a Major League field for the very first time.

The Twins spent the bulk of the 1981 season platooning Ron Jackson and Danny Goodwin at first base. Both players had come to the team from the California Angels, in the Dan Ford trade after the 1978 season. This just happened to be the same period of time when scout Angelo Giuliani signed young Kent Hrbek to a Twins contract. Not only would they find out he could play, but he was also a hometown Kennedy High School product soon to become a legend in Minnesota Twins baseball. When the Twins traded Jackson to Detroit for a player to be named later (Tim Corcoran), it opened a big league roster spot for the Minnesota Chosen One, who had been putting up impressive numbers playing in Single A ball in Visalia, California.

The California League was a hitter's league at the time. I should know because I enjoyed some hitting success of my own, so Hrbek was hardly the only player to put up eye-catching numbers. These same gaudy numbers that landed him a Yankee Stadium debut helped gain him recognition as the Most Valuable Player in the California League for the 1981 season. This distinction was awarded Herbie even though he missed the last two weeks of the league regular season because of his call-up.

The Bloomington native was penciled in to Manager Billy Gardner's lineup as soon as he arrived in New York, batting eighth in the game at Yankee Stadium. After flying out in his first at bat, Hrbek found success in the bottom of the fifth when he knocked in the Twins' first run with an RBI infield single, his first Major League hit. Then with the score tied 2–2 in the twelfth inning, Hrbek led off with a solo home run off George Frazier, which ultimately became the game winner for the Twins.

While all this was taking place at Yankee Stadium, in between Herbie's at bats, he was calling Manager Dick Phillips's phone back in Visalia, providing his former team with a play-by-play analysis of game results against the Yankees and his accomplishments. At one time, a runner from the locker room came into the Visalia Oaks dugout with the latest message: "Herbie just called and said he got to meet Reggie Jackson at first base after Reggie got a hit; he said it is so freakin' loud you can't hear yourself think! It is awesome!"

This situation was so compelling to me because just one day earlier, Herbie and I were teammates in Visalia. Our personal stats were almost identical, and I even excelled in some. Yet Herbie was living his dream of becoming a Major League ballplayer, and I was still sitting in a dugout in the California League 2,870 miles, three

Minor League levels, three time zones, and four years away from the big leagues.

What was of greater significance to me was that Herbie was my friend and the only teammate I had ever played with at the time who made it to the big show. I had actually played with someone who was in the Major Leagues, and interestingly enough, I knew I could play this sandlot game almost as good as Herbie did. Little did I know that my rite of passage to the Major Leagues, regardless of my present circumstances, was just a phone call away!

Chapter 2
Diplomatic Immunity

The 1981 spring training in Melbourne, Florida, could not arrive fast enough. I limped through a terrible first season playing for the Orlando Twins and had every justification believable for a first-year player. You know, excuses like, "I can't get used to the wooden bats after putting up All-America numbers at Vanderbilt using that reliable aluminum bat"; or "I miss my girlfriend something terrible"; or "I had no idea finding an apartment and having to pay utilities could be so stressful."

Honestly, the wooden bat was an adjustment to a new Minor

Left to right: Terry Francona, Pat Dobson, Don Slaught, Joe Carter, and Phil Stephenson.

League hitter. It was a problem trying to determine what wood bat best suited me that would give me maximum bat speed through the strike zone. Some players lucked out and found the perfect bat early on right out of college, yet I would not hit my stride until the second season of ball, playing in the California League. From that season on, I would use a C271, thirty-four inches long and thirty-two ounces in weight, as my weapon of choice.

I had come out of Vanderbilt University as the second catcher in the draft and a third-round pick. I ended up second in career home runs with 49 behind Bob Horner, MVP of the Southeastern Conference, and first team All-America. I was happiest with the Collegiate All-America recognition, not so much for the stature, but mainly because I had friends also on that team: Terry Francona and Joe Carter, whom I met the fall of my senior year while playing for a USA team in Cuba. All the players on that USA All-Star team, who would participate in the Copa Intercontinental de Beisbol, Cuba, took two weeks off from college in early October 1979 to experience a memorable trip.

That was a special group of players, and many of them on that team eventually made it to the show. It was such an honor representing our country and playing on the first American team to travel to Cuba since the Che Guevara–Fidel Castro revolution.

Fidel and Che overthrew the US-backed Fulgencio Batista in 1959, and it has been a one-party state led first by Fidel Castro and now by his brother, Raul, since then. At the time of our visit, the Soviet Union was pumping subsidies into Cuba to the tune of $4 to $5 billion a year. Yet our visit in 1979 displayed to us that Cubans were still living in the late 1950s or early 1960s at best, based on the model and year of the vehicles throughout the city of Havana as well as the crumbling infrastructure. Nothing was being renovated or built. Ten guys would be standing around a ditch with two digging and eight watching while resting on their shovels. There was no motivation to work because there was no opportunity for advancement.

Since the revolution, hundreds of thousands of Cubans had fled their country to go to the United States for a better life. During our ten days in Cuba, it seemed that daily we met a Cuban citizen who would show us a photo of a relative living in America and ask us if we knew the person. Most pictures seemed to be taken in front of the Disney World entrance, and of course, no relatives in the photos were familiar to any player on our team.

We were warned that contact between foreign visitors and ordinary Cubans was de facto illegal, and government officials kept our entourage of ballplayers at arm's length from most Cubans. The people were very eager to approach us and wanted to practice speaking English. They always talked about how great America was and how they so hoped they would one day make it to the United States. Thus, the government frowned upon our conversing with the Cubans hungry to talk with us and tell the truth about living with communism. But they also wanted to tell us about their baseball team, which represented the national pride of their country.

Baseball was introduced to Cuba in the 1860s, and the Habana Base Ball Club was established in 1868. The revolution in 1959 did not do anything to change the Cuban people's love of baseball, and their leader was a baseball fanatic. In fact, if Fidel Castro had been just a little bit better baseball player, Cuba might never have gone Communist. He would have signed to a professional baseball contract as a pitcher and would have more than likely played ball in America at the same time he was plotting a revolution with Che Guevera. Castro and the Cuban government recognized that the roots of baseball ran deep, so they chose baseball as a symbol of excellence and as the rallying cry for nationalism. The government soon replaced the professional for-pay model of baseball with an amateur model driven not by money but by national ideals. Baseball was Cuba's bloodline, by far its most popular sport, and the one that Fidel Castro emphasized.

Even as dismal as their living conditions were in Cuba, none dared utter a bad word about Fidel Castro. I was not sure if he was viewed as a hero to those still in Cuba, or his ability to make life miserable for the dissident, outspoken Cubans weighed heavy upon their opinions. Either way our interpreters asked us not to go off with any Cubans. We were supposed to stay in the hotel and travel only as a team.

That did not mean anything to me. I viewed the government-appointed tour guides' comments as a personal challenge to somehow and some way see the sights and hear the sounds of Cuba. Little did I know that I would get the chance to see the streets of Havana probably like no other American had for many years.

Since we were the first American baseball team to travel to Cuba in decades and since baseball is their numero uno sport, it was only fitting that we were rock stars everywhere we traveled. The people ran to our buses and tried to climb on board. They asked for baseballs, bats, USA ball caps, and even our uniform tops that proudly displayed across the chest USA in bold letters.

Around the stadium, the government protected us with police or military escorts and kept barricades up between the Cubans and us. But one night after a game, for some strange reason as we walked to the buses, the police protection dissipated into thin air, and the barricades came down. There was a mass stampede of Cubans, as many as several hundred, who ran in our direction, causing our entire team to run as fast as we could to the safety of the buses.

The Cubans rocked the bus I was in and climbed through the front door and windows, trying to grab our hats and any memorabilia item that had USA on it or anything else that had something to do with baseball. Several guys had their hats taken off their heads, and we literally had to use baseball bats to hit people and push them away from the windows. I saw Mike Brown, a Clemson product, trying to get his hat back from a fan who had climbed halfway into a back window and stolen Mike's ball cap right off his head. He was so pissed that he started throwing baseballs out the window at the horde of rabid fans.

Jack Stallings, our coach from Georgia Southern, hollered at the bus driver to drive away as fast as he could. We surely ran over some rioters when our two buses sped away with fans holding onto the windows and trying to latch onto the bus as we drove away. It was frightening, and the fun in being rock stars quickly disappeared. We could not believe the mob scene that we had just escaped, and we were gun-shy the rest of the tournament. From that day forward the escort protection doubled, and we never had another problem with the fans entering our personal space.

Our games allowed us to travel all over the country, and we played in several provinces throughout Cuba and outside Havana. When we visited the provinces of Pinar del Rio and either Holguin or Santiago de Cuba, we were sponsored by the national party of Communist women called the Federation of Cuban Women. The government recognized them as the national mechanism for the advancement of women in Cuba. One woman later told me they were formed to "defend the Cuban revolution."

We entered a town either by bus after a long ride or by bus after a short flight and traveled to a secure and gated home or some sort of government housing project. They provided us with a grand entrance, and the local Cubans were gathered to meet the American celebrities. They clapped and shouted as we were ushered in to sit in front of the citizens and hear a speech from a powerful Communist female leader.

From the best I could understand and after several conversations with our interpreter, I learned that the Communist Party was touting progress and emphasized, "Look what we have done for you, and look how far we have come to make all the people equal. We have now brought you baseball as promised, and here is the American team."

I shared my box lunch with these kids.

I certainly didn't see the progress they touted. What I saw were Cubans struggling with little to eat and little hopes that an individual could improve his position in life. If you were a ditch digger at twenty-five, you were going to be a ditch digger at sixty-five too!

At all the events, they served us box lunches. Sitting in folding chairs, we opened our mystery cardboard box lunches only to find a ham sandwich or a ham and cheese sandwich, with a handful of fruit and a bag of chips with no markings on the outside of the package. The bread, although not moldy, appeared quite stale, and the guys just could not stomach eating the specially prepared meal from the Cuban women's Communist Party.

Mike Brown, the Clemson pitcher who was still upset about his hat being stolen, said, "What are we supposed to do with this?" Our best solution, so as not to appear as ungrateful dignitaries, was to take a very small bite and then share the food. The lack of edible appeal was not the only motivator to walk away hungry. While we were being honored by some government dignitary, the local people, especially kids, were staring at us.

We all felt guilty that we had food to eat. The looks in their eyes were those of envy derived from hunger and a desire to eat something tasty. We just could not bear to eat in front of them since we knew their daily struggles living in communism included finding adequate food resources to survive.

From the first day there, I gave away my box lunch to some kid who gravitated toward me using the trickery of a smile. In just a short while every American All-Star was handing out his box lunch, and we became bigger than life, even larger than we already appeared. It made for a joyous time as the children sat in our laps while they ate and seemed to be so happy on the day they met their first American-born ballplayers.

In the mid-1970s Castro started economic reforms, and the people kept talking about what was to come. When we traveled to another province to play, we would be in the middle of nowhere with a forest of sugarcane fields on our right and our left and then suddenly come upon a bridge. This bridge, in appearance, was just the roof of a bridge situated over the highway. Actually, it was nothing more than an overpass for us to drive under. There was no entrance to the bridge from either the right or the left side, and it usually stood out like a sore thumb in rural areas with no road coming off it in any direction.

I asked our Cuban-born interpreter, "What the heck is this all about?"

He spoke to us as if he was telling a secret that would land him in prison or at least some form of punishment, such as being removed from this envied job traveling with us. "Oh, that is progress!" he said. "Our government builds these bridges in the middle of the rural areas to demonstrate to the people that progress is coming. We have named these construction projects the bridges to nowhere."

One of the bridges to nowhere.

The most enjoyable and unanticipated time of our trip was the day we entered a compound to meet more Communist Party dignitaries. A barbed wire fence surrounded the residence, which kept the locals, who were all lined up, outside the premises. Chairs were set underneath tropical trees that provided the entire area with much-needed shade.

In America you could compare the meeting to an all-women's service club that meets once a month to discuss local affairs but serves mostly as a means to get out of the house and find female camaraderie. We listened to the regular welcome speech peppered with Communist Party propaganda, and then there was a lull in the program as a band prepared to play.

To really appreciate the surrounding, you have to visualize twenty-three American ballplayers, in the prime of our lives, in the best condition of our lives, all with beautiful girlfriends back home, sitting on one side of the courtyard. The speaker and the area serving as the dance floor were the only barriers between us and approximately forty women representing the Communist Party in Pinar del Rio. All the women kept staring our way during the speech, and I was all too familiar with that "look." We were about to experience our first and only encounter with Cuban cougars. These ladies were hoping to be able to go home and spread a folktale of how they danced with the American ballplayers and took advantage of the American men!

The Latin band started playing their first song of the day. About halfway through it, I got the idea to make the ladies' wishes come true. After all, this was about our third encounter with these ladies heading up the Communist movement, and they were always smiling at us, none ever speaking English. The pickings were slim to none when it came to beauty, but I was not looking for romance in Pinar del Rio nor was any other American ballplayer or coach. We just wanted to have a good time!

The need for laughter and fun is universal, and dancing just seems to bring out the best in everyone, even if you have two left feet. By the time the second song began, I had walked across the soon-to-be-smoking dance floor and approached the first row of ladies with my hand extended. Here was the first opportunity in Cuba to exercise my Vanderbilt-learned Spanish dialect at a time when it really mattered: asking a lady to dance.

I smiled and selected my partner based totally on her brightly colored blouse with a hint of Latin flare. "Excusamente, que pasa! Quieres bailar?" Bingo, she took the bait, and we were off to dance together to lively Cuban tunes. Brian Little soon followed my bold lead, as did Kevin Shannon.

Soon the guys who were still shyly sitting in their chairs needed not to worry, for these women were on the prowl. Evidently, the women at this function thought it was quite proper for a woman to ask a man to dance, and they were fighting each other to snatch the nearest USA All-Star baseball player and drag him to the dance floor. The cougars began to pounce on their prey, and most of the ladies sprinted across the courtyard and started grabbing players.

Everyone, including the coaches, ended up on the dance floor sometime during the festivities. We were all laughing and carrying on like we were celebrating the end to all grievances between Cuba and the USA.

The funniest sight was Mark Dempsey of Ohio State dancing with his partner. Mark at six feet, seven inches towered over her; she was about five feet nothing and as round as she was tall. Mark just laughed and laughed, and it was a memorable and joyous time for the women who were proud members of the Federation of Cuban Women.

We took one flight to another province outside Havana, and somehow during the flight I became friends with the pilot. I'm sure it was because I gave him some gift that was a token in my eyes but must have made an impact on him. To this day I believe his name was Raul, but it doesn't matter because he was the face representing all the dissidents in Cuba who were too afraid to be outspoken against Fidel Castro.

Upon leaving the plane, Raul had offered to meet me and told me he would come and see me in a couple of days. True to his word, he visited our hotel two days after our trip, but he was not allowed in the hotel to wait for me. The rule was that only guests from out of the country could enter.

I had forgotten his offer; I never took him too seriously anyway. One afternoon following morning practice, I left the protection the hotel provided its guests to venture across the street to buy some ice cream. I was embarrassed when I found Raul patiently waiting to greet me and take me on an adventure.

He had waited for three days off and on to see me! After I sincerely apologized for not looking for him earlier in the week, he offered to show me the city. I was eager to take the chance with a complete stranger and see where our trip would take us. I expected to climb in the front seat of a car, so I was totally surprised to see a

Cuban cougar on the prowl.

Mark Dempsey with his dance partner.

Raul, the pilot of this plane, took me around Havana. Oddly enough, Craig Lefferts is waving in the foreground. I hit my only Major League home run off him.

motorcycle with a sidecar parked around the corner from the hotel entrance. Proudly parked behind a 1957 Chevrolet was a Harley-Davidson flathead with sidecar. It looked to be a WWII vintage or a police model. Raul said his family brought it over from Puerto Rico before the revolution in 1959. It was the coolest form of transportation I had ever ridden in, and it came complete with a funky helmet and some eye goggles.

I hopped in the sidecar, hunkered down, and off we went through the streets of Havana. On the ride, I just kept leaning in the opposite direction from the way it felt like we might tip over. If someone from the government had the job of keeping track of the American ballplayers when they left the hotel, that person completely failed that day. Remember, this was 1979 and Americans were not allowed free rein in Havana, Cuba.

Raul introduced me to every relative he had in Havana. First, we met his mother and father. They didn't speak any English; there was no need for them to ever learn a language other than Cuban Spanish since they weren't allowed to go anywhere. His two sisters heard that Raul was with the American ballplayer, and soon both siblings and their families all gathered around the outside of his parents' simple home.

They wanted to talk about their lives and their living conditions, which were the same as everyone else in Cuba, other than high-ranking government officials. Raul interpreted for all of us. A main topic was the desire to have access to more consumable items. They lived at what would be the poverty level in the United States. They were allowed one gallon of milk, four loaves of bread, and two pounds of meat a week. All the family members voted in the last election for Fidel, the only choice on the ballot. By voting, each participant received a free pair of government-issued shoes. Since every Cuban citizen needed shoes, the participation of voters at the polls was close to 100 percent.

It was later in the trip when I arranged to sell them our blue jeans. American-made blue jeans were a fashion statement in Cuba, and they sold on the black market for $200 US a pair. I convinced the guys on the team to sell their jeans, and each guy walked away with $80 cash in his pocket. Raul insisted on paying for them, so it was a win-win when capitalism marched on the streets of communism in the form of Levi jeans.

The conversation ended with the most important subject, baseball. They all loved the game and told me they were honored to have such a baseball dignitary visiting in their home. Even with that said, they hoped the Cuban national team would win the tournament. Pride in your national baseball team helps you forget the atrocities of life!

After we left his parents' home, Raul took me past the national library, hospitals, apartment complexes, and statues honoring Fidel's fighters in the revolution. It was a special day for me, and

'57 Chevys and our motorcycle with its sidecar.

I learned firsthand what books could never teach me. People are just people no matter where they live, and the same desires, needs, and wants are universal. And of course, baseball is still a game that brings people of differences together.

I gave my address to Raul and his family and invited them to visit me if they ever made it to America, but I never heard from them.

Fidel Castro's entrance into the stadium for the very first time during our tournament play was memorable. We were playing in the Estadio Latinoamericano, the grandest baseball park in all of Latin America. It was a spacious park, adored by pitchers since the Caribbean tropical winds were always blowing in from the outfield. I guess that is why I was somewhat proud of my home run I hit during the Copa Intercontinental de Beisbol play against Japan.

You had to really hit a ball square to get it to leave the yard in Cuba and, in particular, in this stadium. The field surface was big league quality, and the lighting system was Major League quality as well.

It was the largest stadium I had ever played in, holding some

Copa Intercontinental de Beisbol, Cuba '79.

55,000 rabid Cuban baseball fans. It was originally built in 1946 but was renovated and expanded in 1971. I guess Soviet Union money actually did do some good for the people of Cuba! The stadium was a monument and a testimony to the love of baseball that both Castro and the Cuban citizens felt for the game.

The grand stadium was packed the day we played the host team, and the Cuban fans were hollering, "USA! USA! USA!" when we walked onto the field prior to game time. My emotions began to overwhelm me because everyone was standing up and waving and cheering for us. I felt like we were walking out of the tunnel in Yankee Stadium and our own American fans were pulling for their favorite team.

It seemed like within a matter of minutes, however, the chants quickly changed. Their revolutionary leader, Fidel Castro, entered the stadium and acknowledged the Cuban faithful. The cry echoed throughout the stadium, "Fidel! Fidel! Fidel!"

I was warming up the starting pitcher that night, who happened to be Ken Daley; Ken was the pill-throwing left-hander, who later found the rotation of the St. Louis Cardinals. In Cuba, players actually warmed up the starters between the dugout and home plate, the pitching mounds set at an angle, with each respective team staying on its side of home plate, yet not more than fifteen yards apart from catcher to catcher. As I heard the roar, I looked up to see this large figure of a man wearing his trademark puke green army fatigues—tailored, of course—and carrying an impressive cigar in his left hand. He appeared to be walking right down to meet me. The only obstacle Fidel would have to overcome to shake this All-American's hand was the backstop situated between him and me. Fidel stopped short of the screen and found his seat directly behind me, a mere fifteen to twenty feet away.

You could tell he had charisma; leaders of his stature just stand out in a crowd. There was something about him that gave him the appearance of being important. He was certainly fit, and his aura exuded extreme confidence. He knew he was special, yet he gave off this air that he was friendly and approachable.

Something immediately came over me as I thought, *I'm taking Spanish II at Vanderbilt this semester, and it might be a good time to impress someone of importance.* So I dropped my mask, walked right toward the Communist leader with my hand outstretched, and boldly spoke Spanish not much better than an illiterate sugar cane migrant. Well, either my Spanish was better than I thought, or Fidel was in a friendly mood because the Cuban leader stood up and placed his right hand through the screen to welcome me to Cuba.

The crowd again erupted with "USA! USA!" and the soldiers ushered the rest of the team over to meet Senor Castro. I certainly never supported his policies, but Fidel was another of the many interesting people I would meet in my baseball travels. My desire to talk to a head of lettuce later prompted Pete Rose to name me the "Mayor." Castro's appearance later in our dugout after the game made for a good night at the yard, even though the USA players lost 2–1 in a great ball game.

Fidel in the
stadium dugout.

Before I move on from Cuba, another interesting story involves superstars familiar to people who follow baseball. We young American players were quite bored in Havana, since we were restricted to our hotel; and besides that, there was nothing to see and nothing to buy in any store. I can attest that Tom Joad and his family ate far better in Steinbeck's *Grapes of Wrath* than any Cuban under communism ever did.

Bored college baseball players usually find trouble. Thank goodness we never got caught with this prank, or we might still be in Cuba, and the Boston Red Sox never would have won a World Series and the Braves would have beat the Toronto Blue Jays. We were staying in the Hotel Habana Libre, and besides practicing or playing baseball, the highlight of our day consisted of walking across the street to a famous ice cream parlor, the Coppelia. So, we could order helado in the day and cervezas at night, which was the only way we could spend money in 1979 in Cuba.

One evening, Joe Carter from Wichita State, Terry Francona from Arizona, Kevin Shannon from Texas, Brian Little from Texas A&M, and I were together in someone's hotel room. Most of you know who Joe Carter and Terry Francona are, but Brian would see some show time with the White Sox. His brother Grady Little was the one-time manager of the Red Sox and Dodgers. Strangely enough, Brian was about to initiate a prank with another future manager of the Red Sox, Terry Francona.

Other players were coming and going in the evening, and just when we reached an all-time boring state, Brian "Twig" Little entered the room. He was carrying a water balloon and laughing in a devious way. It would be the first of several balloons as the night strike force was beginning its assault. He sounded like Dick Dastardly's dog Muttley laughing, and he had the guilty look of a rule breaker that stretched across his face.

These water balloons were so large that we couldn't throw them with our hands. No, we had to place them in the middle of bedsheets and sling them over the railing with a guy holding each end of the sheet. The first one we catapulted hit the pool deck just below, where a swarm of people were socializing around the pool. When the balloon hit the pool deck, it sounded like an explosion, and people scattered everywhere. Some people even fell into the pool because of the panic created by the sound of impact.

The USA All-Star strike force later moved to a more strategic offensive position in the hotel, which overlooked the main street below. That was both stupid and exciting as we launched at least three balloons onto the congested street filled with Cuban pedestrians. Soon armored military personnel pulled up to the scene of the crime and shined lights onto the hotel windows.

Oh, did I forget to mention that we were on the twenty-third floor of the hotel? I guess looking back, we could have hurt someone if a direct hit occurred, but we college ballplayers in a foreign country actually believed if we got in trouble, the United States would pull out all the stops to rescue us and might even send in the

Balloon drop zone.

Marines to bail us out. We justified our false sense of importance as US representatives playing on foreign soil, so we figured we had diplomatic immunity.

Just a few weeks after that trip to Cuba, beginning on November 4, 1979, fifty-two Americans were held hostage in Iran for 444 days. If we had known ahead of time about the possibility of Americans being held hostage anywhere in the world, that would have effectively ended our balloon hurling before the first one was tossed.

The end of the venture occurred the next day when we walked across the street to get our daily intake of ice cream. I canvassed the street and saw the scattered remains of the prior night's balloon bombing. I carefully confiscated all the pieces and squirreled them away in my pocket. Then at a picnic table in the park, as all the guys enjoyed their ice cream, I showed them the crime scene evidence and read the words printed on the balloons, *Texas A&M Aggies*. And you wonder how those Aggie jokes get started?

Chapter 3

Brophy vs. Fraley

Back to the Twins spring training yard. After a dismal first season, I was in negotiations with the Twins over my 1981 season contract. The Twins were notorious for squeezing every dime out of their players, and their philosophy was no negotiations, period! What they send a player is normally under the heading of "you take it or don't come to camp." Their chintzy philosophy started at the top with Mr. Griffith.

I met the Twins' owner, Calvin Griffith, during the summer of 1980, sometime around the month of August. Baseball was in Mr. Griffith's blood. He was raised by his uncle Clark Griffith, the Hall of Fame pitcher and president of the Washington Senators, going all the way back to 1920. Clark passed on in 1955, and the team became the responsibility of Calvin. Under Calvin Griffith's ownership, the Senators were moved to Minneapolis-St. Paul, Minnesota, in 1961 and renamed the Minnesota Twins.

He operated under old school philosophy even for 1981. He financed the Minnesota team solely on revenues he took in from the gate and concessions and was the only owner who relied on baseball revenues for a living. There was no TV market per se in Minnesota, and his attendance figures were always last or next to last in the league. His livelihood outside of baseball was dependent on what was left over. So, he was not aggressive about acquiring high-salaried free agents, for that affected his take-home pay. He believed in the game of baseball that involved sacrifice bunts, great defense, solid pitching, and a big league team developed from within the organization. He was not into the entertainment business of high-salaried stars, so free agency just irked him.

Mr. Griffith was famous for some of his sayings ("He'll either be the best manager in baseball—or the worst," he once said when he gave young Billy Martin his first manager job). Unfortunately, one of his most infamous remarks landed him in trouble in 1978, drawing charges of racism. Speaking at a Lions Club dinner in Waseca, Minnesota, Griffith was quoted as saying: "I'll tell you why we came to Minnesota. It was when we found out you only had 15,000 blacks here. Black people don't go to ballgames, but they'll fill up a rassling ring and put up such a chant it'll scare you to death. We came here because you've got good, hardworking white people here." His comment was not too carefully thought out, especially when his team fielded a black player named Rod Carew. But you do have to admire Mr. Griffith. Although he held a silver spoon throughout his young life, he earned his way to the top, working first as a batboy and then climbing up the ladder within the organization and holding every position in a baseball organization.

Word came to me to report to the offices at Tinker Field in Orlando; Mr. Griffith wanted to talk with me. I believed Mr. Griffith wanted early on to personally meet all his players, and this was his way of checking my pedigree right out of the box. It started as a pep talk that included Mr. Griffith's desire to encourage me to attend Instructional ball in the fall in order to enhance my baseball skills.

In response, I kindly informed him that it was my desire to complete my college degree in the fall.

Mr. Griffith said that there was plenty of time for that and then asked where I was going to college.

When I stated, "Vanderbilt," he replied, "You really should finish your education, so I think it is a good idea for you to go back this fall to Vanderbilt."

I never saw him again, but I knew from Mr. Griffith's response and his complete change of mind-set during the meeting that my choice of a college institution was dead-on perfect.

Once you pulled on the purse strings from Mr. Griffith, you then had to wrestle with George Brophy. Now you're talking about a hard-ass when it came to contracts; he was the poster child for one-way negotiations. My agent, Robert Fraley, learned that early on in his career, unfortunately at my expense.

You may remember Robert, for he had an impeccable reputation as the head of Leader Enterprises, yet was mostly remembered by his clients and personal friends as the man who tragically died with Payne Stewart in their airplane crash on October 25, 1999. Robert's sports career began as an Alabama quarterback under Coach Bear Bryant, starting a few games and later finishing his education with a tax degree at the University of Florida.

Robert was a deliberate, slow talker, and his looks were a cross between Opie Taylor and Robert Redford with biceps. He soon became a sports agent but not just your average agent. He was a true friend of those he represented, including the likes of Bill Parcells, Joe Gibbs, Bill Cowher, Ray Perkins, Bill Curry, Steve Sloan, Frank Thomas, Payne Stewart, and Orel Hershiser for starters. I was proud of the fact that I was the one who introduced Robert to Orel Hershiser just prior to Orel's fantastic pitching years, an incredible find for Robert. The two outstanding, godly men would become best friends, a match from heaven as agent and player. Other genius moves were getting Payne to dress out of the NFL box and later encouraging Joe Gibbs to build a racing team.

Several years after Robert's death, I spoke to Coach Gibbs at the Talladega Racetrack and asked him about Robert. With his head bowed Coach spoke softly and said, "He was my friend and I miss him dearly."

I met Robert in my senior year at Vanderbilt. My mentor, the late Dr. Lee Minton, was our mutual friend who facilitated the introduction. Without a doubt, I was Robert's first client, and he cut his teeth negotiating with George Brophy.

When I was fresh out of college, "All Everything" in baseball at Vanderbilt, Robert got me a whopping $15,000 signing bonus from the Twins. Later, he would be the same guy who convinced the NFL to pay Payne Stewart $600,000 to wear those silly ass NFL team–colored knickers on the PGA Tour, and he would get Orel

Twins, Scotti Oceans Apart In Negotiations

By JOE BIDDLE
Banner Sports Writer

Scotti Madison, Vanderbilt's first collegiate All-America baseball player, got his first taste of professional baseball Wednesday and found it a bitter pill to swallow.

Wednesday afternoon Madison was informed the Minnesota Twins had selected him in the third round of the annual amateur summer draft and Fred Waters, who had tutored Madison in Little League, would drop by his parents' home in Lillian, Ala. to discuss a possible contract.

Waters' visit did nothing to boost Madison's morale. The Twins' notoriously frugal owner Calvin Griffith, has refused to bow to the escalating salary structure employed by a majority of major league teams.

Water's initial offer was one Madison could, and did, refuse. Flatly.

"I'm not really encouraged at all," Madision said today by telephone. "The Twins rank 22nd out of 26 major league clubs on average salaries and it's easy to see why. There's no way I can sign for what they offered. It would be hard to get by on. We're a pretty good ways apart."

Madison, unaccustomed to the intricacies of negotiating a professional contract, will seek legal advice from a family friend. He plans to meet with Waters again tonight.

"I don't like the first offer at all," the Vandy catcher said. "I'm not going to sign my life away that easy. But I don't know how all this works. I don't know if I'm their (Twins) property now or not."

The Twins have promised Madison he will be assigned to their Orlando (Fla.) farm club of the AA Southern League, an opponent of the Nashville Sounds.

★ ★ ★

a $3,000,000 payday with the Dodgers, which at the time was an unheard of amount. Yet he was so frustrated after his dealings with Mr. Brophy and so embarrassed that he had obtained so little riches for me, he said he would represent me for free.

Robert was available as needed, but I never again asked him to negotiate a contract for me. I said, "Just give me some guidance." And really, what good could an agent of Robert's skills accomplish with a future big league career .163 hitter? The player must have some talent for the agent to negotiate some money, and not even Robert was a magician. When it came to negotiating with the Twins, he admitted, "Talking with George Brophy was harder than pulling teeth."

So I would be handling the big negotiations with the Twins in the upcoming spring of 1981. I figured I had attended Vanderbilt, played two sports, and actually graduated in the fall of 1980 after maneuvering with Roy Kramer, my athletic director, to pay for my last nine hours of school. Coach Kramer became the commissioner of the Southeastern Conference (SEC) and the godfather of the Bowl Championship Series (BCS) for college football. Coach was quite the man, held respect from everyone near him, and was the ultimate motivator and negotiator.

The strategy I used with Coach Kramer was what I planned to use in the upcoming negotiations with the Twins. See, once upon a time I walked into Coach's office the first week of September, arriving right after my first season in professional baseball, yet a little late since classes had already been in session for a good week. I told Coach Kramer that I needed financial assistance to pay for my last nine hours of education and that I could not afford Vanderbilt since the Twins had almost stiffed me with an embarrassing $15,000 signing bonus.

Just three months earlier Coach Kramer and his fun and entertaining wife, Sarah Jo, witnessed my teammates and me win the SEC championship in Gainesville, Florida. So, they were well aware of my decorated past at Vandy.

After my well-thought-out request, Coach proceeded to remind me that Vanderbilt had fulfilled its responsibility to pay for four years of college, and I did not have any eligibility left in any sport, baseball or football.

Managing to wiggle the conversation my way, I told Coach that I could not take these needed classes because they were offered only in the afternoons, and since I played baseball and football, I was always on the field either practicing or playing every afternoon the entire four years.

Coach was unrelenting on the eligibility issue, but I sealed the deal when I stated with a sad look on my face, "Coach Kramer, wouldn't it be a tragedy if Vanderbilt's first All-American in baseball didn't graduate?" Coach didn't hesitate; with a sly smile on his face he immediately sent me to see the person in charge of financial aid. Because of that success, I felt that I was seasoned enough at negotiations and was ready for the Twins management. Or so I thought.

The same Mr. Brophy who had gotten the best of Robert Fraley was notorious for not negotiating on ballplayers' contracts back in the day. Now, the modern-day Minor Leaguer playing with the Twins and probably every other team operates under a sliding scale. If you are in Single A ball and you have played so many years, you make X. If you are in Double A ball and you have played so many years, you make XX. Everything is on a spreadsheet, so there are no second-guessing and no negotiating.

But in 1981 when I walked into the Twins camp at the Melbourne Airport, every contract was unique, and everything was negotiated to an extent. The negotiations went something like this: you received a contract in late January from the Twins telling you what you were going to make, and then you would call Mr. Brophy and speak to Jim Rantz. The purpose of sending out the contracts so late was to give players minimal time to cause management a problem. Mr. Rantz would say something like, "What we sent you is all you're going to receive, son!"

This went on, back and forth, for several weeks, and as spring

camp approached, the last message was, either you sign the contract we sent you, or you will not be issued a uniform to wear in
practice when you get to camp. Well, 99 percent of the guys were
signed before they stepped foot on those cow pasture fields in Melbourne. Then there was me.

Jim Rantz was a dedicated employee, totally faithful to Mr. Brophy. My experience with him happened early on in what would
become his storybook career. He is the poster child for professional
baseball when it comes to longevity. Rantz's baseball roots ran deep
in the state of Minnesota, beginning when he pitched the University of Minnesota to a victory in the 1960 College World Series and
signed a professional contract with the Senators, soon to be Twins,
a few weeks later.

During his playing tenure, his shoulder began to bother him,
and in 1965, George Brophy, the Twins assistant farm director,
called to see if Rantz might want to manage their St. Cloud team in
the Midwest League. Rantz viewed this as an opportunity to keep
him in the game by throwing some batting practice to determine
his playing options. His shoulder never responded well, and Jim's
chances of playing in the Majors ended. After the Northern League
season ended, Rantz approached Brophy for a job in the Twins front
office. The Twins were in the process of winning the pennant and
would be hosting World Series games, so Rantz began by working
in the public relations department. The job became permanent by
the following year. Little did anyone know back then that Mr. Rantz
would become a baseball lifer.

In 1970 after farm director Sherry Robertson was killed in a car
accident, Brophy moved into his spot. It paved the way for Rantz
to become Brophy's assistant. While still an assistant for Brophy,
Rantz was responsible for the Twins learning about Kirby Puckett,
who played for the Quincy team in the Central Illinois Collegiate
League in 1981.

In 1986, Brophy left the Twins, and Rantz took over as director of Minor League operations, a position he still holds. He has

the third-longest-running tenure in professional baseball with the same team. He has remained with the Minnesota Twins organization for fifty-five years, since their inception working as a player, a manager, and finally a front office person, all of which sent him into the Twins Hall of Fame.

☎

Back to the 1981 Twins spring training. This particular season I wanted a raise, surely not because I had torn up the Southern League the summer before, but because I had played for $700 a month and felt that a contract of $900 was more in line with my talents. When I received the offer from the Twins, a whopping $700-a-month salary for the 1981 season, I couldn't believe it since I had just come off a season making the same $700-a-month salary playing Double A baseball in Orlando. I thought, *Have they even heard of a cost-of-living increase?* Almost delirious with frustration, I immediately went through Ma Bell (readers of a certain age: Ma Bell was the nickname for the telephone company) to express my displeasure with what surely was an honest mistake and contacted the Minor League offices.

Over the phone, Mr. Rantz and I went round and round about the $900-a-month contract. I caved a little and asked for just a $100-a-month raise to bring the salary up to a nominal $800 a month.

Rantz told me in no uncertain terms, "Mr. Brophy agreed to pay you $700, and our policy with the Twins on second-year players is that we do not lower their salaries the next season, even after only half a season of performance."

I craftily fired back, "Well, considering I'm making the minimum of $700 now, it is impossible to lower my salary any more since I am already at the very bottom of the pay scale. So, I'm asking for a $100 raise to bring my salary up to a more attractive level."

There was no way that was going to happen under Mr. Brophy's watch. To allow that would create chaos for all future negotiations if word got out that the Twins caved to Madison.

Just a week before spring camp started, Mr. Rantz called me and said that if I did not sign the contract, I could not come to spring training. I told Mr. Rantz the Twins' offer of $700 a month was an embarrassment to anyone who had ever attended Vanderbilt University.

The final message from Rantz on the phone was this: "The bottom line is that you will not receive a uniform unless you sign your contract, regardless of your choice of colleges!"

Trying to reason the comment away, I said to myself, *So what? I don't need a Twins uniform. I have plenty of baseball gear to practice in. In fact I still have my old Tate High School uniform, and it fits me like a glove. I'll wear that uniform in camp, and once they see me play, they might even give me a $200-a-month raise just watching me hit.* To this day, you can be assured Mr. Rantz had no idea I would even show up to camp on March 12, 1981, without a signed contract, much less in a hodgepodge uniform.

Within a day, I would make the trek from Lillian, Alabama, a small bay town adjacent to Pensacola, to Melbourne, Florida. The entire way there I worried about my "no contract" status and prayed under my breath that my comment to Mr. Rantz did not come across as smart-ass college graduate arrogance. Insolence just might impede my chances to make it to the Major Leagues before I ever made my first spring training appearance.

Chapter 4

Granny

Before I left Pensacola for the long trip across the upper half of Florida, I stopped to say good-bye to Granny. If you had a grandmother or a mother who provided the spiritual backbone for your life, you can relate to the relationship that I had with Granny. She was a praying Granny, the kind who always prays for her kids and grandkids, no matter how old they are or where they are in their walk in life. She had the direct phone number to Oral Roberts and called him often. I was fortunate to enjoy the love and support of three grandmothers over the years, and the other two—Bama and Mom—both loved baseball. They were always encouraging to

Scotti and Granny.

me and wrote many letters of comfort during my Minor League days. Yet Granny provided the stories of laughter that are a topic of conversations to this day.

My granny was quite the character, and my roomies over the years often answered the phone in the mornings to hear my Pensacola grandmother on the other end of the line. I never figured out how she could track me down on all those road trips in places like Edmonton, Canada; Columbus, Georgia; Spokane, Washington; Amarillo, Texas; and Syracuse, New York.

Granny rang the room looking for her grandyoung'un and always proceeded to talk with my roommate for the next ten minutes, finding out everything about him. Once my roomie was Dale "Home Team" Holman of Louisiana fame. After Dale sleepily answered the phone and spoke with her for thirty minutes in a hotel room in Vancouver, Canada, I thought it was Dale's grandmother on the phone until he asked me, "Did you get the Vienna sausages your granny mailed you?"

Granny obviously knew how to navigate around Ma Bell, and she always knew where I was during the season. That is, until I went to Dodgertown and failed to call her and update my playing status and, most important to Granny, my spiritual status. That would be when Granny got the best of Dodgers Manager Tommy Lasorda, which probably prompted Tommy to pull the ultimate spring training trick on me later in the spring camp of 1982.

☎

Now it was early in camp, about two weeks into the Grapefruit League season of 1982, and I was asked to travel with the team to a spring game away from Vero Beach. My role that day was nothing more than to catch batting practice prior to the game, yet I was really excited to be able to travel to a game where paying fans and coeds packed the stands with the sole intention of seeing their favorite Dodgers stars. That day I wore the Dodger number of 79, the perfect numeral if I had been starting at right tackle for a football team on that particular March day. But in baseball, the extremely high number indicated only that my importance to the Dodgers was slightly less than insignificant.

The Dodgers were just coming off a championship year in '81, and their draw at ballparks was second to none. I knew the park would be packed with sun-seeking fans, and my work would end in the batting cages before the game with only a slight chance that I might warm up the starting pitcher. I was hoping that would be the case since the Dodgers ace that day was traveling with them. Fernando would be pitching for them, and the bus was loaded with many other big-time stars as well.

The 1981 Los Angeles Dodgers season had gotten off to a strong start when rookie pitcher Fernando Valenzuela pitched a shutout on opening day, starting the craze that came to be known as Fernandomania. Fernando went on to win both the Rookie of the Year and the Cy Young Awards, so his presence alone was bringing fans to the park.

The 1981 season was odd because of the baseball strike; the season was divided into two parts since the players went on strike in midseason. The guys on the bus were discussing the past season with distaste, and all were hoping that the 1982 season would be the customary one long continuous season, not a divided season. The '81 Dodgers won the Western Division of the National League in the first half and advanced to the playoffs. They beat the Houston Astros in a divisional playoff and the Montreal Expos in the National League Championship Series before beating the New York Yankees to win the World Series.

The bus was carrying the remnant of the championship team, and I sat by the All-Star first baseman, Steve Garvey, exactly five seats back from the front on the right side, by the window. Garvey was nicknamed "Mr. Clean" because of his squeaky clean image during his National League career. Sadly, that name would not stick when Garvey's personal life became a soap opera in the mid-1980s. As a ballplayer he excelled, winning MVP honors in 1974 and being selected a ten-time All-Star. He batted and threw right-handed, and in a nineteen-year career, Garvey was a .294 hitter with 272 home runs and 1,308 RBIs in 2,332 games played.

I liked "Popeye" as I secretly nicknamed him due to his large forearms. Garvey was always nice to this batting practice catcher, treating me with great respect every time he spoke with me. It would end up being Garvey's final season along with the great third baseman, the "Penguin," Ron Cey. Both were on the bus that day along with Steve Sax, the future Rookie of the Year for the upcoming 1982 season.

While I was talking to Garvey, no more than ten minutes outside the confines of Dodgertown, Tommy Lasorda began to dominate the conversation in the front of the bus. He was addressing Vin Scully, the "voice" of the Dodgers, who was across from his aisle seat sitting directly behind "Bussie" (the affectionate name every team gave its bus driver). Scully was already a legend and would soon win every award a broadcaster could possibly win and even earn a star on the Hollywood Walk of Fame.

I was trying to carry on a conversation with Garvey and at the same time eavesdrop on Lasorda's discussions with his retinue of baseball legends. Shortly after what seemed to be Lasorda's boisterous attempt to bring everyone on the bus into his conversation, he instantly caught my attention: "Hey, is Scotti Madison on the bus today?"

Immediately I swallowed my tongue and gasped for air. Not saying a word, I was singled out by Steve Garvey, who politely said, "He's right here!"

Lasorda invited me to the front of the bus and began to tell the following story: "Yeah, last night I am in bed with my wife, Jo, and the phone rings. This lady at the other end says, 'Hi, I am Scotti Madison's granny and I haven't heard from him in a couple of weeks and I was just wondering how he was doing?' So I then spoke to her like she was my own grandmother for the next twenty minutes. Scotti, when you get home today from this game, go back to your hotel room and call your granny so she won't wake me up again tonight and ask how her grandyoung'un is doing!"

The front of the bus erupted in laughter, and I walked back to my seat, red face and all. Once I made it back to Dodgertown I did as he said and called Granny from my hotel room: "Granny, I was wondering how you got Tommy Lasorda's number?"

She replied, "Well, son, I was watching the news, and it said Tommy Lasorda was the head man of the Dodgers. Since I hadn't heard from you in a while, I wanted to see how you were doing so I decided to get on the phone and track this Tommy Lasorda fellow down."

"Granny, you can't be calling my manager in his hotel room. The next thing I know you'll be calling Peter O'Malley to check on me."

Granny quickly responded, "Who is he?"

I knew I better leave it at that because Granny had a real knack for tracking down the decision maker everywhere I traveled in baseball. Neither I nor Granny ever met Peter O'Malley and Granny never called him, but I was fortunate enough to meet other owners in my travels while I was participating in the sport known as America's pastime.

Chapter 5

She Does Have a Heart

Over the next ten years, I had the opportunity to meet many Major League owners during my travels from the Minors to the big leagues and then back down again. I admired all of these baseball owners for the hard work they endured in order to build their empires in a variety of fields ranging from fast-food pizza delivery to real estate to the automotive industry. I met Calvin Griffith, owner of the Twins, at Tinker Field in Orlando, and Avron Fogelman, owner of the Royals, at a picnic on the ball field in Fort Myers, Florida. Yet the two owners who left lasting impressions on me were Tom Monaghan, owner of the Detroit Tigers, and Marge Schott, owner of the Cincinnati Reds.

This Vanderbilt graduate was smart enough to know that if a young and ambitious college graduate can grab a few nuggets of wisdom from overachievers, they might serve me well in my life. These people not only had good days in their lives; they had good lives when you looked to the very core of their essence. Yes, there was controversy, and yes, they were criticized in the press. But remember, "People always throw rocks from the back of the line forward."

☎

In the spring of 1985, I had the privilege of dining with Tom Monaghan during the Tigers big league training camp. Monaghan owned the Tigers from 1983 to 1992, and during that period, Domino's Pizza invited its top managers from across the country to Lakeland, Florida. The company hosted a dinner, and as a perk for the managers who exceeded Domino's sales quotas at their respective store locations, Mr. Monaghan invited Detroit Tigers to mingle among the high achievers at the recognition dinner. Tigers players did not have much of a choice about whether to attend. We came in from a day of practice, and those of us who were selected had an invitation at our lockers placed nicely on our chairs: "The Detroit Tigers would like you to attend dinner with Domino's executives tonight at 7:00 p.m. Your attendance is appreciated!" They meant that our attendance was expected and mandatory.

Although attendance was mandatory, I actually liked the idea since it was a free meal. I was trying to save money for the long upcoming regular season. It also gave me a chance to meet and mingle with some overachievers in the Domino's empire, including Mr. Monaghan.

Thomas Stephen "Tom" Monaghan (born March 25, 1937, in Ann Arbor, Michigan) is an American entrepreneur and dedicated Catholic, who founded Domino's Pizza in 1960. He started with nothing, built an empire, and later used his money to promote many conservative movements including the Thomas More Law Center, a public interest law firm dedicated to promoting social conservative issues. The issues the Law Center pursues, mostly through litigation, are generally in line with modern American social conservatism: opposing same-sex marriage; opposing pornography; supporting pro-life positions and initiatives; and opposing the removal of the Ten Commandments and other religious monuments from municipal and school buildings.

You often wonder what motivates people to do great things or give back to those who are less fortunate or support a cause important to them. It usually begins from something impactful occurring in early childhood and is often grounded in deep moral conviction in God, in family, in dedication, in perseverance, in conviction, and in hard work. I always enjoyed meeting successful people who had paid their dues and had reached the pinnacle of their professions, yet still possessed the humility to treat others with dignity and respect.

Mr. Monaghan was such a person, and his early childhood experiences formed the basis of his desire to give back to society. A

September 25, 1989, article written by Peter Alson and Julie Green-walt for *People* magazine tells us about Monaghan's upbringing:

> When Tom was 4, his truck-driver father died of a perfo-rated ulcer. His mother, who Tom believes "couldn't stand" him, was studying to be a nurse and didn't feel she could handle two toddlers, so Tom and his brother, Jim, 2, were shunted off to foster homes and then to a Catholic orphan-age. A brief reunion between mother and sons took place when Tom was 12, but it wasn't long before his mother banished the boys to foster homes once more. (Monaghan and his mother did reconcile before her death last year. "She did the best she could," he now says.) . . . There was never enough money to make Tom feel secure. "I was always embarrassed by my poverty," he says. "I dreamed of better things." After graduation he enlisted in the Marines. But there was haplessness even in that bold move. "I thought I was joining the Army," Monaghan admits. "I got the recruit-ment centers mixed up." He realized his mistake as he was signing up and decided to live with it. He's glad he did. "If I could survive the Marines," he says, "I knew I could handle anything." Today Monaghan, who has four daughters— Mary, 26, Susan, 24, Margaret, 20, and Barbara, 17—swears that if he had a son, "he wouldn't get a penny from me until he spent two years in the Marines."

There always appear to be suffering and hardships in the lives of many great achievers, and these difficulties help mold the char-acter of someone as influential as Mr. Monaghan. Your success is determined by how you respond to defeat, and Mr. Monaghan re-sponded well. Most important, he kept God in his family's life.

I met his daughter Susan when I played for the Nashville Sounds, then the Triple A team for the Tigers, and she was a testa-ment to his legacy. Susan Monaghan was in her early twenties at the time, an attractive woman, soft spoken with a good heart. She was interning for the Sounds while I was catching in Nashville, and we would talk at the ballpark and meet a couple of times after Sounds games and visit at one of those late-night dining spots the Music City is noted for. I really enjoyed her company, and I could tell she had deep roots grounded in conviction. Susan told stories of her dad's work schedule when Dad first began with a couple of pizza joints. Mr. Monaghan would work all day, make it home in time for dinner, and remain home a couple of hours, so he could put Susan and her sisters to bed. Susan said, "Dad would say our prayers and give us each a kiss, and then he would head back to work and close the pizza parlor, making it home after midnight. For Christmas last year, Dad filled up a plane with food and toys and took the whole family to Nicaragua to give the poor a Christmas."

☎

It's easy to understand why Tom Monaghan left a lasting impression on me. He lived the talk! At Mr. Monaghan's award dinner in Lakeland honoring his Domino's managers, I had the opportunity to leave a lasting impression on Mrs. Al Kaline, the wife of the great Tigers baseball player. It would be a different impression from the one Mr. Monaghan left on me!

Only one time was I able to join the Domino's elite for dinner, and my seat at the table happened to be right next to Al Kaline's wife. The famed Tiger was seated just one seat over to her right. In 1953, Al Kaline bypassed the Minor League system and joined the Tigers team directly from Baltimore's Southern High School as an eighteen-year-old bonus baby signee, receiving $35,000. His father was a broom maker, and he feared he would follow in those footsteps, so he put everything he had—time, energy, and hope— into baseball. He never played in the Minor Leagues, and once he joined the Tigers out of high school, he played the next twenty-two years as a Tiger and played in eighteen All-Star games. In 1955 at the age of twenty, he won the batting title with a .340 average;

he was the youngest player to ever win the American League batting title.

I first saw him play when I was in the fifth grade. The teacher brought in a TV so we could watch the World Series during class time. He was bigger than life that day, and I remember him hitting off Cardinals right-hander Bob Gibson, a Hall of Famer. Now, I was getting a chance to sit near a man who was a hero in my boyhood dreams.

No salacious scandal has ever tainted Al Kaline's name. Never has there been the slightest suggestion that he used performance enhancers to juice up his baseball numbers. He never received a large multiyear contract. His life was pure and simple: same life, same wife, and baseball was his first love. He was a legend in professional baseball, and I was well aware of his nickname, "Mr. Tiger." He was a true gentleman and a superb athlete. He was the second greatest Tigers player with only Ty Cobb leading the way—barely. I was also aware Al Kaline never spent one day in the Minor Leagues, and I was now playing in my fifth grueling season traveling to all my games on a second-rate bus. This guy never sniffed a Greyhound bus!

Al married Madge Louise Hamilton in 1954, and she was the epitome of the faithful wife. I knew she was quite proud of Al because she talked about the Hall of Famer the entire night. Madge asked me about my career to date, and I wasn't sure if she was genuine in her questioning of my well-traveled Minor League career. I felt her probing was a means to bring up the fact that Al never played in the Minor Leagues, "How long have you played in the Minors? You know, Al never spent a day in the Minors!"

This line of questioning and bringing up the Tiger great's lack of Minor League playing time went on throughout the evening, and after the fourth "Al never spent a day in the Minor Leagues," I had enough. In a kind way, I addressed Mrs. Kaline head-on with her bragging explanation of Al's jump from high school directly to the Major Leagues: "You say Mr. Kaline never played in the Minor Leagues."

"That's right. He never did!"

"Mrs. Kaline, I am so sorry to hear that Al never played in the Minor Leagues. I wanted to say something earlier, but I just couldn't bear to address such a sensitive subject. It is a real shame your husband never traveled through the Minor Leagues. I have been in the Minors for five seasons, and I have found them to be the most wonderful years of my life. Your husband sadly will never be able to enjoy such a wonderful experience like I have cherished being a Minor League player. How sad that he went right to the big leagues."

Mrs. Kaline looked at me in disbelief and turned her head in Al's direction for the remainder of the dinner. I knew that was the last time she would discuss Al's career with me. It would also be the last time I ever sat at a table with Mr. and Mrs. Al Kaline. I was okay with that, and I knew it was the only perceived advantage I would ever have on Al Kaline's professional baseball career. It was also the last time I was ever invited to a Domino's Pizza awards dinner. The food really wasn't that good that particular night!

☎

In the spring of 1989, I would again be a nonroster player invited to spring training, and this time the Cincinnati Reds were sending out my invitation. The Reds spring training facility was located in Plant City, Florida, and it would be their second season in the Strawberry Capital of the world, after relocating from Tampa, a home they enjoyed from 1946 to 1987.

Although destined to start the season in Triple A, this eternal optimist always believed I had a chance to make the Major League club from spring training. The nonroster players stayed in the Holiday Inn in Plant City, adjacent to the interstate. The rooms were average in quality, yet they could have been worse. At least they were clean, and I didn't have a roommate the first couple of weeks, so I liked the independence granted me by the Reds and the quiet time it afforded, which I often needed to escape the business of baseball.

My first two weeks at camp consisted of catching pitchers and taking some swings in the batting cages as well as off live arms on the mound. I enjoyed hitting off the Reds aces like Ron Robinson, Tom Browning, Jose Rijo, Danny Jackson, Kent Tekulve, Rob Dibble, and John Franco. After batting practice, I ran some for conditioning or lifted weights, depending on what day it was in my workout routine.

Always after a half day of baseball, I headed to the Holiday Inn pool, caught some rays, and maybe wrote a letter to a family member, friend, or business acquaintance. I was selling insurance for Aflac in the off-seasons, and I wrote letters to customers during spring camp to inform them of my playing status. Over the years I found out that many of the recipients saved those letters. I hadn't realized just how many letters I had written during spring training to my clients and prospective customers. There is something special about receiving handwritten letters, and I learned this forgotten art of communication early on in my career. I must have written hundreds of letters during my ten seasons at Florida spring training facilities, and besides being the proper way to keep my friends abreast of my status, it probably helped my insurance business immensely.

This particular day I found a poolside table covered by the shade of an umbrella. It was a slightly overcast day, and the pool, oddly enough, was completely vacant, except for one lone guest sitting under an umbrella at the far end of the pool. I grabbed my seat and placed my writing tools on the table. I glanced up to look more carefully at the lady and soon realized it was Cincinnati Reds owner Marge Schott. I had only seen her on television prior to that day, but she was easy to recognize, sporting her out-of-style wardrobe, reddish in color. And then her dog was lying underneath the table at her feet.

Why not meet my boss? I stood up and walked her way. I visited with Mrs. Schott for the next two hours in complete privacy, and by the end of the conversation, still no one else had come to the Holi-

day Inn swimming pool that weekday afternoon. I felt as if it was
meant to be, a private conversation with the most powerful woman
in baseball. There were few women in executive positions of Major
League baseball during this period of time. There were certainly no
female owners, so Marge Schott was in a category of her own.

I learned a lot about the character of the Reds owner: what
made her tick, and what were the core values driving this highly
controversial and ruthless business legend. Mostly I learned that
Marge was a very compassionate person underneath those rough
edges. What the world seemed to know about her was a totally
different person from the woman I met. Rightfully so, the press
stereotyped her due to her battle axe mannerisms and racial insen-
sitivities. However, I believe they overlooked her upbringing and
her heart for baseball fans of Cincinnati.

Marge Schott was a proud third-generation German-American
and the managing general partner, president, and CEO of the National League's Cincinnati Reds franchise from 1984 to 1999. She
was the third woman to own a North American Major League team
without inheriting it.

Her popularity as a Major League franchise owner was surpassed
only by her controversial behavior during her tenure as owner of
the Reds, which included slurs toward African-Americans, Jews,
the Japanese, and homosexuals. In November 1992, Tim Sabo,
a former employee of the Reds, was suing the team and accused
Marge of referring to Reds outfielders Eric Davis and Dave Parker
as "million dollar niggers." The accusation was brought out in a
deposition, and Sabo alleged he was unjustly fired because he op-
posed the Reds' unwritten policy of not hiring blacks. Marge was
tainted from that point on, even though she was exonerated in this
court case when Sabo lost his lawsuit.

Charles "Cal" Levy, a Jewish man and another employee, alleged that Schott kept a Nazi swastika armband at her home and
claimed he overheard her say, "Sneaky goddamn Jews are all alike."
The next day, Schott issued a statement saying that the claims of

racism levied against her were overstated and that she did not mean to offend anyone with her statement or her ownership of the armband. Schott attempted to explain away the swastika armband as a remembrance of her late husband's heroic efforts during the Second World War. According to Marge, in his service to his country he had saved a fellow soldier's life. In gratitude for this act the soldier had given him the souvenir Nazi armband as a token of appreciation. More than likely, since she grew up under a staunch German father, it was something she had acquired during her childhood. After all, she was a hoarder who never threw anything away.

Marge got in more hot water when she stated in late November 1992 that the "million dollar niggers" comment was made in jest. Moreover she did not understand how the epithet "Jap" could be offensive. During the same time frame, another baseball assistant from the Oakland Athletics stated in a *New York Times* article that she overheard Marge say, "I would never hire another nigger. I would rather have a trained monkey working for me than a nigger."

In February 1993, Marge was fined by baseball $250,000 and banned from day-to-day operations until November 1, after the 1993 season. Then Marge opened her mouth at the 1994 Ohio County Treasurers Association, "I do not want my players wearing earrings, because only fruits wear earrings. I was raised to believe that men wearing earrings were fruity." This was also during a time Marge reluctantly rescinded the long-standing Reds' policy that prohibited facial hair, after meeting with the newly acquired and bearded outfielder Greg Vaughn. She later fired manager Davey Johnson during the middle of the season, and the rumor was that she did not approve of his living with his fiancée prior to their getting married.

Her outlandish and inappropriate actions and comments continued to sprinkle the landscape of baseball with the final nail in her coffin being hammered in on opening day of April 1, 1996. The Reds were hosting the opening day game, as was traditional to baseball, and inclement weather in the form of snow battered

Cincinnati earlier in the day. Before the game started, umpire John McSherry collapsed face-first on the field surface and died before he reached the hospital. The other umpires postponed the game, denying the fans of Cincinnati a ball game, and it was their first cancellation of opening day in the Reds' storybook history. It was a bad day all around. Marge was shown to be visibly upset, and her comments centering on "unfairness" were heavily criticized. In her eyes she was taking up for the loyal Cincinnati fans, yet to her critics, she was again insensitive to those not sharing her beliefs.

Her comments, "Adolf Hitler was good in the beginning, but went too far," and "I hate to see Asian-American kids outdoing our kids in high school," were the last straws in the eventual collapse of her Reds ownership.

That spring day of 1989, I sat with Marge for what seemed like a lifetime, listening to her concerns about baseball and the state of affairs of the Cincinnati Reds. When I first introduced myself as a new Reds player, oddly her opening question was, "Did you finish college, hon?"

I mentioned my degree from Vanderbilt, and she asked me to join her. She said, "Honey, it would be nice to have an intelligent conversation with one of my ballplayers." She had a lit cigarette in her hand, and the rest of the pack was open on top of the table adjacent to a glass of something, most likely vodka. It was not that I was all that smart or that I had the correct answers to her questions; I served as a means to relieve her conscience that spring afternoon. I was just "an ear" for Marge as she called me "honey" and "hon" while unleashing a lifetime of personal hurts surrounding the game she loved.

Marge began to speak in a grating tone as if she was talking through sandpaper in her mouth, "I am running a business in a man's world, and they don't want me in baseball. Who do they think they are, telling me how to run my team? No one tells anyone how to run their business, but since I'm a woman, they make a big deal out of everything I do. They don't say anything about George Steinbrenner or how he runs the Yankees. The powers that be in baseball are going to do everything they can to get me out of Cincinnati. When I bought the team, no man in the city stepped to the plate to buy the team. I wanted to keep baseball in Cincinnati."

She then proceeded to tell me about how baseball was questioning her solution to Kal Daniels's contract dispute. Earlier in the week, on March 3 to be exact, Kal and Marge walked into the Reds' parking lot to solve his contract dispute. Kal had not played long enough to qualify for salary arbitration, so he had no options, and his salary was at the mercy of Marge Schott. He had just come off a season hitting .291 with 18 home runs and wanted a salary of $325,000. Marge was not willing to pay that, and she suggested they just settle it with a coin toss. Marge called "heads," but the toss indicated "tails." Kal left the parking lot richer and walked into the locker room to inform the team he won the coin toss. Pete Rose thought it was the coolest way he ever saw a salary dispute settled and congratulated Kal.

Marge caught flak from Major League Baseball about her means of resolution, and she told me at the swimming pool, "This is my team, and I will decide how much I pay my players and how I determine that. If I want to toss a coin, I will toss a coin. I should have called tails!"

I had to agree. It was her team, and it ultimately was her business, so why did the commissioner's office really care that she flipped a coin?

She then discussed how important it was to give the fans the best possible team at the lowest possible ticket cost. Marge said she was faced with a real dilemma; she believed everyone regardless of economic condition should be able to see the Cincinnati Reds play. It just didn't sit well with her to charge these fans exorbitant ticket prices to see a baseball game. She stated, "I want to charge a fair price and I probably undercharge, so I can't bring in the money to get big-time free agents. I am in a real pickle here!"

Listening to Marge vent, I added an occasional "yes, ma'am" to the end of her topic.

She looked at me with serious concern and said, "I just can't figure out why Johnny Bench and Pete Rose don't get along! You'd think they would be best friends after playing together and winning a championship. You know, pride is a bad thing!"

I didn't know anything about that comment then but learned a little more about the two Hall of Famers after being called up during the middle of the 1989 season. It was then I learned that Johnny Bench and Pete Rose did not get along and, in fact, despised each other. It seemed to be common knowledge in the locker room and was similar news on the streets in Cincinnati. One time Tim Leary and I played golf at one of the country clubs where Reds players were given perks, and that day the golf pro was in a tizzy. He told us that both Pete and Johnny called him and both wanted a tee time at the same time. He was freaking out in front of Tim and me and insinuated a fight might break out in the parking lot if he couldn't straighten out this tee time with Johnny and Pete. Both superstars had streets named after them, and I just assumed that the city of Cincinnati had enough room for only one superstar in the eyes of these two baseball legends.

Next Marge talked about women's role in the workplace: "There are a lot of problems that occur when women leave home and get a job. Women really have no place in baseball and certainly not in the locker room like some of these hoochie-coochie female reporters who walk right in under the cover of press! Who do they think they are kidding looking around at my players! And then some of them wear sunglasses to boot!"

I did chirp in on this topic, and I agreed that women reporters had no business in a male athletic locker room: "They don't allow men reporters in the women's locker room. It is a total double standard in sports reporting."

At that comment she asked if my father was still alive. I loved my dad and found out that my dad and Marge's father had a lot of similarities. Both were very tough men, each with a heart buried beneath the pain of living. Both grew up very poor and very hard.

Marge said her father never showed his children affection, but he taught them discipline, the value of a dollar, and that hard work can accomplish just about anything. He was very strict, and the five sisters received plenty of disciplinary action while growing up. He had plenty of friends and seemed to treat others in the community even better than he did his immediate family. Most of all he said to them, "You better be tough because you are women in a man's world."

I could relate to the toughness and the spankings. One time after meeting the legendary Hall of Fame football coach, Auburns' Pat Dye, I told Coach Dye that my dad was Charlie Madison, who played with his brother Wayne Dye at Georgia.

Coach Dye said, "You are Charlie Madison's son? He was the meanest man to ever play football at Georgia. I idolized your father."

The other disciplinarian in my life was Uncle Carl. Uncle Carl, or "Coach Madison" as most knew him, has more wins than anyone else as a head coach in Florida high school football. He was also tough on me, and he taught me to practice hard until it hurts, for then the games are easy.

So both my dad's life and my uncle Carl's life were never short on discipline, and just like Marge's father, they preached mental toughness. Dad always reminded his son, "It doesn't matter what you did last game; you are only as good as the next game you play!"

Marge appreciated how I was raised, and she seemed to grow into her seat even more comfortably at the poolside table while lighting another cigarette every ten minutes. She ended our conversation with her dislike for Chris Sabo.

It was only because of Chris Sabo's injury that I was called up to Cincinnati during the 1989 season. I never had much to say to Chris, and "Sabes," as some on the team called him, never spoke to me one time during my brief experience with the Reds.

Once I was on a bus with Sabes, and the Reds had just completed a spring training game during Grapefruit League play. Sabo had a fantastic 1988 season, and he was awarded the Rookie of the Year honors after posting a .271 average and stealing 46 bases. Thus, his popularity had skyrocketed in just one season, and the fans at spring training wanted a piece of the Reds star third baseman. I believe talking with the fans and signing autographs come with the territory of enjoying athletic fame. I could never figure out why some players were so adamant at telling fans no upon their request for an autograph. Maybe in a private setting with your family, a "No, not at this time," would be an acceptable response. But at the ballpark, your autograph came with the price of admission.

Sabo entered the bus, and a couple of young girls who were following him stopped at the front entrance of the bus and hounded him for his signature on their newly purchased Reds souvenir baseballs. Sabo, who was halfway to the back of the bus, turned completely around and headed back to the front steps, then yelled at the girls, "Get out of here. I am not signing any autographs and don't ask me again. Get lost!"

Signing autographs for the Tigers.

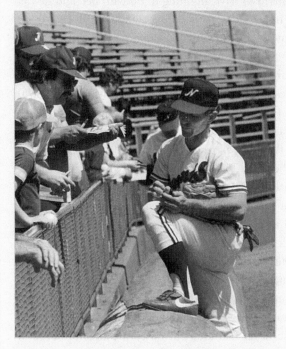

Signing autographs for the Royals and the Nashville Sounds.

Sometimes I wonder if in later years when the fame has diminished to a mere flicker of candlelight, do those players who once turned their fans away, crushing their perception of their idols, now wish someone would want their autograph just one more time?

Marge started in on her attack of Sabo: "That Chris Sabo just rubs me wrong. You know I had a banquet that all the players had to attend, and I specifically told them it was mandatory to wear a coat and tie. Chris comes to the banquet in a pair of blue jeans and a blue jean jacket. I was so embarrassed, and I could not believe he totally defied me. I had a lot of Cincinnati businessmen in attendance, and I expected my players to dress the part of Cincinnati Reds players. He looked like white trash at this event.

"You know when he made it to the big leagues, his lady friend came to Riverfront driving a station wagon and pulling a U-Haul trailer? Sabo refused to have anything to do with her, and he told her to go back home. Now he is dating some floozy! That is unacceptable behavior! He just got too important for her after she stayed with him the entire time in the Minor Leagues."

Then she launched into the subject of men who were unfaithful to their "significant others." I don't know if that was the case with Chris Sabo and I was not there at the banquet; these were Marge's comments. But any hint of infidelity regarding any player upset her, and she chided the guilty party.

Looking at her past, you can understand why she was so disturbed over marital unfaithfulness. In 1968, after sixteen years of marriage, she inherited her husband's massive automobile dealerships, as well as his interests in other industries when he died of a heart attack while sitting in the bathtub of his mistress, Lois Kenning. Charlie Schott left Marge everything, including a broken heart, but he taught her never to trust.

Marge was only thirty-nine at his death, yet she never married again. Most spouses never get over unfaithfulness and understandably so. She also never had kids but raised a couple of dozen St. Bernards as a substitute for children. Marge probably never could trust another man again, so it is easy to understand her sentiments toward men with wandering eyes. She was proud to say she was trying to get rid of the "cutesy-poos," her name for the baseball groupies who ended up in players' hotel rooms. To accomplish her goals of policing unfaithfulness, she had Reds personnel videotape her players coming and going off charter flights and team buses to make sure the cutesy-poos were nowhere near her Reds players when they entered the hotel. It sounds a little like methods practiced by the German Gestapo!

The last incident between Marge and Sabo occurred during a team meeting in Cincinnati in 1989. I was on the big league team at the time, and the Reds were in the middle of a soon-to-be ten-game losing streak. The *Cincinnati Enquirer* was blasting the team's performance, and we just weren't playing that well.

Prior to batting practice, Pete Rose, our manager, told us to get dressed and head upstairs for a meeting with Mrs. Schott. "Players only," Pete hollered out. This assembly of ballplayers was certainly unusual, and in all my days of playing baseball, I never experienced a team meeting that was "closed door" and called by the owner involving just an owner and his or her players.

We had no idea what Marge wanted with us, but we all headed to the top of the front offices, walking as a team underneath the stadium. It took three runs of the elevators to get all the players to the executive

Scotti in the Reds uniform.

boardroom, and once everyone found a seat in the large conference room, it got real quiet. We were engulfed with the color red, and we felt like we had entered the gates of hell, each player staring at the others and wondering whose soul would be on display today.

Marge was the last to enter the room, and her sidekick, Schottzie, a St. Bernard, was walking just ahead of her. Marge's dogs were famous for having their run of the place around Riverfront Stadium. You could look up and see them almost anywhere wandering throughout the park. It was a commonplace for them to find the field's artificial surface as the best place to defecate around the stadium.

The dog settled at Marge's feet as she began to question our performance of the past week: "Guys, we have hit a rut, and we are not playing very well right now. We have a seven-game losing streak right now, so what is going on? I would like to hear from the team as to why we aren't winning!"

For a little while there was an awkward silence. Finally, some of the leaders addressed her concerns. The first to begin to explain away our losses was John Franco; then Tom Browning, Eric Davis, Ron Oester, and maybe Paul O'Neill chirped in with the same sentiments. The upshot from them was, "Mrs. Schott, we're playing as hard as we can. We have had some key injuries, and we're catching everyone hot when we play them. It's just baseball and the way the ball bounces sometimes!" The truth was spoken, yet the bottom line was, we just weren't that good.

When Marge provided her final insight to the team, our meeting ended abruptly: "Guys, look, I don't seem to have any answers as to your poor play, and you don't have any answers about why we are losing. Have you all thought about getting together as a team and just praying about it?"

Her morally correct suggestion took us by surprise, and before anyone had time to take her seriously, Chris Sabo delivered his opinion. He was directly facing Marge, who was sitting at the end of the boardroom table, and he was adversarial in his response,

"Marge, what the heck! You got a guy at the plate praying to get a base hit and you got a guy on the mound praying to throw a strike. Who is going to get the prayer?"

Marge peered down to the opposite end of the dark shaded boardroom table; the room was completely quiet as the players were looking for a hole to hide in. If looks could kill a Reds player, Chris Sabo would have been six feet under. Marge rose to her feet, seemingly disappointed, and vocalized her final sentiments to the Reds ball team as she walked out of the room, "This meeting is over!"

We looked at each other and quietly headed back downstairs to play the Padres and lose another game—our eighth loss in a row, with two more losses soon to come.

There were more topics in the one hundred or so minutes I

Scoring against the Braves.

spent with Marge. She left only because she finished a pack of Carl-ton 120s. She raised her head to me and said in her raspy voice, "I'm out of cigarettes! It was a pleasure to meet you, honey. It is so nice to meet a Vanderbilt graduate in baseball! I hope you make the team!"

It didn't matter to me that she had not remembered my name and she called me "hon" most of the time. Here was Marge Schott, an often cold, calculating person, who sometimes was very mean spirited, displaying a softer side that day, a woman with a heart. That doesn't excuse her actions or her words—and I do not defend them—but there was a place in her life that showed concern for others. Through her words on the pool deck of the Holiday Inn, I recognized why Marge was Marge! She would go on to help many less fortunate in distress and would do everything she could to as-sist the economically challenged in her hometown.

Marge Schott led a very lonely life, no matter from what angle you looked at it. The men in her life enriched it and blessed her, but they also broke her heart. The character of Marge Schott was formed through her disappointments in secular love.

Although she was cold to men, she had a big heart for animals and children. At Riverfront Stadium, she would come to the game early and scour the stands to find some fifteen to twenty kids, and she would then walk them out on the artificial surface and let them run to the center field wall and back. Another story has her visiting the opening day of a Little League for disabled children, and Marge cried the entire time at their difficult plight. She seemed to be great to everyone's families, but to those in her inner circle, such as her employees and the Cincinnati Reds players, she often came across as spiteful. If you really think about it, Marge Schott, through the crass business side of baseball, had become her father!

Chapter 6
Big Fella

U pon arriving in Melbourne in the spring of '81, I was excited to enter the locker rooms for the first time and hurriedly selected a locker with as much privacy as you can get with 150-plus players in small confines. It was my first day to meet Kent Hrbek. Our lockers were down the side by the back wall in the clubhouse. Kent was much larger in stature than I was, kind of "howdy, howdy" looking, built like a modern-day Abe Lincoln. There were other players certainly bigger than Kent around the shoulders and chest, but he carried himself well enough to be considered a big guy. He loomed even larger standing in the batter's box, and when he swung a bat, he was Goliath.

Kent Hrbek, 1981.

From the first day we met, Herbie always called me "Chuck." I thought he acted a little carefree, almost goofy at times, but soon I was the goofy-looking one to everyone in camp.

I quickly settled into my new home by strategically placing all my gear around the locker. The smell of sweat was etched in the cement confines and got considerably stronger as the spring training days wore on. Years of players had come and gone, and the whispers of felled dreams seemed to speak from every corner of the locker room. It was a dismal setting and needed not only a new paint job but also a good scrubbing. Better yet, an atom bomb placed in the center of the room would serve it justice. It just wasn't a warm and fuzzy clubhouse like the one I had known at Vanderbilt. No, it served its purpose, as a place to quickly come and go. Everything important to your career was outside the doors, and this was only a place to dress for battle.

After setting up my gear, I walked out of the locker room, wondering if I had what it took to survive this camp and be selected to play on a team. It would be my first spring training, and I was quite nervous about the first practice the following morning.

☎

At Twins camp, the morning of March 12, 1981, was a Thursday, as if it mattered. Every day was the same in the life of a baseball player. The only difference today was that it was opening day camp, so the anxiety was higher than normal. What else could you possibly feel with a big group of ballplayers standing in line for breakfast, staring each other up and down and wondering, *Damn, he's a big guy. I wonder what position he plays?*

Whatever hopes you might have had that a good, hearty breakfast would ease some of your tension quickly dissipated upon sight of the Twins Minor League breakfast buffet. In all of my travels I had never seen such an embarrassing display of food. Then it proceeded to get worse after tasting it! The bacon had so much

TWINS AIRPORT MOTEL
MELBOURNE REGIONAL AIRPORT
1060 JOE WALKER ROAD • MELBOURNE, FLORIDA 32901
(305) 723-5440

March 17, 1981

Dear Tim,

I hope all is well in the Music City and I know the insurance is going well. It would sure be a plus if some of my groups will open for you. I can't believe the Cats! What happened? Oh well, Kyle Macy sure was needed.

Presently I am practicing with the Triple A team, but I think they will send me some- where else by the time the season starts. I really don't know what to think except to go out there and bust ass. There is about 160 guys now, so 60 has to be released - like killing flies. This is also giving me a chance to brush up on my Spanish for about 20 of the guys here can't speak English. I'll be here for about 3 more weeks, and then I'll give you my new address - Tell everyone hello.

Best Wishes,

The wondering agent -

Scotti

grease on it that the bread underneath the bacon used to soak up the bacon grease actually floated in the pan. They fed us powdered eggs, and the scrambled eggs were always watery, so they used a spatula with strainer holes in it to serve the players. We used to try and work the cafeteria staff to slip us real eggs on the side. Tim Teufel was the best at sweet talking, and it seemed that one of the work staff took a liking to him. He worked the relationship and somehow ended up with real eggs at least twice a week. He was our Morgan Freeman (in his *Shawshank Redemption* role) at Twins spring camp.

The toast was piled so high that you thought it must be a newly designed Lego set in disguise, and the cool temperature of each piece of bread forced holes in the bread when you attempted to spread the butter. The milk and orange juice were considerably warm, almost puke warm, so room temperature water became the drink of choice for most guys. Honestly, the USA team ate a far better breakfast in Cuba than the one served at the Twins Melbourne Airport spring training facility.

What made it even worse was looking out the window while eating. We could see Calvin Griffith's nephew, Bruce Haynes, practice chipping next to the cafeteria. He seemed to be living the good life decked out in his pastel Izod shirts while punching a few wedges at this imaginary green. We all said, "Are you kidding me? We are eating a breakfast designed for refugees, and this guy is getting ready for his round at the country club?" It made it hard to swallow our morning meal.

One spring training into the future in 1982, I would find out at Dodgertown how the rich and famous lived, a far cry from the Twins camp. On that side of the track you could eat eggs any way you ordered them. You had all kinds of fruit, pastries, and even salmon and bagels as options. They must have set out three different types of juices and the same number of choices in milk from chocolate to skim to whole. It was like a Disney vacation at Dodgertown compared to the Twins' prison food. Even as bad as the breakfast was every day in Melbourne, the stress of trying to make a club out of camp overshadowed the poor quality of the meals.

☎

At the Twins camp, the first day after breakfast I walked to the clubhouse, actually looking around to see if armed guards walked throughout the facility. A few Barney Fifes policed the area, mostly to see to it that we stayed away from the airplanes parked near the ball fields. I found my locker, and a feeling of contentment swelled up within.

Anyone who has ever played a sport knows the feeling of security and peace when you sit near your locker. It's your personal space and becomes your home for a considerable time. It contains all your stuff, and that stuff is all you have and all you need. My baseball gear was my "Linus blanket," especially the catching gear. A famous Linus quote was, "Never jump into a pile of leaves with a wet sucker." Well, I can tell you, "Never show up at spring training without a contract." That was where I was on my road to the big leagues, and I pondered just how this first day would turn out.

I watched everyone proudly putting on his Twins uniform, getting ready for the first morning session and practice day at the yard. Although focused on the business at hand, everyone was in a carefree mood. Laughing and other signs of joy echoed all around: old friends from earlier teams even as far back as college were catching up; guys already picking at each other. It was the first day of spring training, and everyone starting today began afresh.

The uniforms issued at Minor League camp were of quite heavy wool material, and you knew from the occasional minor hole or loose stitching that those uniforms were veterans of spring camps. These were the Minnesota Twins hand-me-downs, yet even as poor as they appeared in quality, I wanted badly to wear one out of the clubhouse that morning. I did my morning business prior to putting on my uniform because I really did not want that many of my peers to see me walking in the locker room in an outcast uniform.

Some say that "the uniform makes the man." I was hoping to turn it around so that "the man makes the uniform." I was about to embarrass myself, and I didn't even know it.

☎

A similar embarrassing uniform incident happened to me at fifteen years of age. I was playing American Legion baseball (ages fifteen to eighteen), and my team was the Greenville, Mississippi, Eagles. We would be playing a doubleheader on a Saturday in Jackson, Mississippi. I was unaware of this city vs. country rivalry that existed in Mississippi; Jackson was the city, and Greenville was the country.

To make matters worse, I was trying out for the Greenville team, and all the uniforms were already spoken for prior to this doubleheader. I showed up in white baseball pants with a red stripe down the sides, a shirt with green sleeves, a fashionable royal blue belt, and a black-and-yellow Cat Heavy Equipment baseball cap that my grandfather let me borrow. My appearance was over the top, even for the country guys from Greenville!

I did not see myself any differently that day, and even with all the catcalls coming from the other side of the field related to my ridiculous appearance, I let performance on the field speak for my worthiness. That day to the best of my recollection, this Pensacola native had two singles, three doubles, and a home run batting from both sides of the plate, besides making all the plays at shortstop. The opposing side had little reason to make fun of me after the game.

After arriving home in Greenville that evening as I was exiting the bus, Coach Skeeter Fleming softly said to me, "Son, you need to come to practice a little earlier tomorrow. We need to fit you in a uniform."

☎

Back at Twins camp, some six years later, I walked onto a field completely out of uniform again. I swelled up with envy when I

Playing for the Greenville Eagles.

saw everyone proudly walk out in Twins apparel. Suddenly, I was overcome with excitement as an idea popped into my head! I could easily blend in if I performed calisthenics from the back of the group. All of the players would be looking the other way, and this positioning could be easily accomplished if I was the last player to leave the locker room that morning. Also, if I hustled more than everyone else, my disparate uniform would appear incidental. Players would have to say, "Wow, this guy really hustles! Who cares about his uniform being different?"

Now looking back some thirty years, I know that it was quite obvious one would see more than 150 players and coaches in dark blue and gray uniforms with dark blue caps lettered with *TC* across the front, and then there was me in a white uniform trimmed in red with the words *Tate High* across the chest. I couldn't find my matching hat, thus my last accessory was a green John Deere baseball cap. I looked as if I was playing in a Christmas baseball tournament, with the colors of the day being green and red.

I once read that during the Civil War, as the war was coming to a close, the Confederate soldiers suffered dire conditions at best. In order to prevent hypothermia from occurring, some were forced out of sheer survival to wear the uniforms of dead Union soldiers into their next battle. Today, I stood out like one of those unbecomingly dressed Confederate soldiers, and I soon was shot down on the battlefield and ushered to the Twins Minor League offices for a face-to-face with Mr. Jim Rantz.

Just as I had carefully orchestrated, I made it through calisthenics somewhat unnoticed. Other players were worried about their own lot, and I don't think they had a second thought about what I was wearing that day, but the coaches reported me to upper management. As soon as players broke to scatter to individual fields, trainer Wayne Hattaway met me on the field.

☎

Wayne had been my team trainer in Orlando seven months earlier, and to say he was a character is an understatement. It is really hard to describe Wayne; his appearance is so unique. I recommend you go to the Internet and look up images of Wayne Hattaway. See what I mean! He looked like a cross between a skinny Yosemite Sam and Yoda of *Star Wars*.

I can't imagine him having any official classes as a trainer, at least not back then. The Twins were not up to spending money for a trainer. It was far more important to have a guy who was first and foremost a clubhouse guy, who could wash uniforms and keep the locker room manicured. Wayne was an excellent clubhouse guy, diligently cleaning everything, but a poor choice for a trainer.

He was fun in nature, he always worked hard, he could pass out aspirin, and he tried to wrap ankles, much to everyone's displeasure. But if he ever saw blood, look out! The Twins were playing a game once, and a guy slid into second base and broke his ankle such that the bone was protruding out of his skin. Wayne ran out to second base and was about to apply his cold spray, a favorite remedy. But as soon as he saw the bone protruding through the skin, he passed out right there on the spot, falling headfirst into second base.

His nickname was "Big Fella" because he called everyone "Big Fella." Wearing an Alabama shirt, a Twins cap, and *Star Wars* socks almost daily, he slapped his leg while talking to you. He defended rassling and Bear Bryant with equal fervor.

Wayne and Chino Cadahia, born in Havana, Cuba, in 1957, just two years before the Castro revolution, often wrestled in the training room. Wayne to this day thinks rassling is the real deal, so Chino played along with him. Chino grabbed Wayne, and Big Fella proceeded to place Chino in the menacing sleeper hold. Chino laughingly begged for mercy, and Big Fella would have none of it. The match ended with Chino either asleep on the floor or effectively neutralized in a slumberous state on the training table. Of course several players witnessed the event, and one would kindly slap Chino on the face to revive him. Chino would complete the final episode admirably and come to his senses remembering absolutely nothing. Big Fella once again walked away undefeated with his championship belt in hand. This was one way we entertained ourselves in Orlando in the summer of 1980, holding a wrestling match once a week.

Wayne was one of the more experienced trainers in spring training and ventured out of his comfort zone to find me on the practice field. Of course I was easy to spot, and Wayne hollered, "Big Fella, Mr. Rantz wants to see you. You can't be on this field practicing without a Twins uniform on."

I nervously left the field, stride for stride with Big Fella, then headed for the dreaded red carpet.

Mr. Rantz met me with one-subject questions: "What's with this uniform? Didn't we tell you that you would not get a uniform unless you signed a contract?"

I politely replied, "Yes, sir, you sure did. But you didn't say anything about me wearing my own uniform and practicing, so I just decided to come to practice."

"Well, son, let's get this contract signed."

This unsigned player tried to convince Mr. Rantz to base my salary on future accomplishments, not according to the past season. Set the salary according to upcoming production with incentives. If you produce, you make money.

Jim axed my idea instantly. I never could figure out why you would not want to pay people based on their results, like a commissioned salesman. It is the American way to pay for performance, yet every professional team steers away from it.

Mr. Rantz agreed to a $50-a-month salary raise and an $800-a-month salary if I made it to Double A. Jim told me that Mr. Brophy might fire him for doing that and made me promise never to tell another Twins player what had occurred.

I never did tell anyone about the Twins concessions with that massive $50-a-month increase. With the pressure of a contract now behind me, it was time to get to the real business, making a club from camp.

If the truth be known, I would have signed for meal money. It was still a game to me and to all of us, and the business of baseball still had not completely set in. The sound of laughter in the locker room, the feeling of accomplishment after a good day, the camaraderie built on similar dreams, the smell of cut grass and pine tar—all of that was what I lived for. What else did a baseball player really need?

Chapter 7
Bleeding Dodger Blue

A fter the first few days in camp, they began to break the players up by position, and all the catchers gathered up at home plate on one field. Each of us was to have four to five throws to second base, one at a time with every other catcher looking on. There must have been fourteen catchers, and it was quite intimidating for me. I was not the smallest in stature, but certainly ranked in the thirtieth percentile as far as my size compared to these other Goliaths standing around home plate.

My arm strength was better than average this spring, yet not long after camp broke, I began to have shoulder problems. The problems lingered for several seasons until I was able to see the Dodger team physician, Dr. Frank Jobe. Dr. Jobe, along with Los Angeles Dodger PT expert Pat Screenar, put me on the very first rehab exercises for shoulder problems in professional baseball.

On field four that day guys were throwing baseballs to second base, and none appeared to have shoulder malfunction. Just ranking their throws, I placed about eighth, which was the middle of the pack, and I just hoped the next seven catchers ahead of me couldn't hit their asses with both hands offensively at home plate. I would have to rely on what came natural, hustle and more hustle, and then whether I could hit! I had been told all my life that if you can hit, they will find a place for you to play.

When we broke up into teams, Herbie and I were practicing with the Mud Hens, which was the Triple A squad of the Twins. After days of practice, Herbie and I were shining at the plate, and we discussed making the squad and starting off in Triple A Toledo, Ohio. The manager was Cal Ermer, best described as a laid-back fellow. If Cal ever got mad at someone, the guy certainly deserved it. Even then Cal never uttered an angry comment, and he probably had as much composure as anyone you could ever play under. Cal liked both of us but was especially fond of Herbie. Just looking around at the caliber of players, I was sure we were shoo-ins to play for the Mud Hens.

I failed to realize, due to a lack of spring training experience, that there were forty men on a big league roster and several nonroster invites to Major League spring camp. They were in Orlando, and when big league camp ended, twenty-four players were going north, and twenty or so players were traveling back to reality, Minor League spring camp in Melbourne. Thus the trickle-down effect occurs, and everyone starts getting knocked down a notch or two on teams.

Herbie and I were predestined to go to Visalia before camp ever began. The two of us were written on the big chalkboard, located somewhere behind closed doors, with the team listed, Visalia Oaks, above our names, well in advance of battlefield accomplishments.

☎

Eventually, I learned a lot about this trickle-down effect when I was invited to my first big league spring camp with the Dodgers a year in the future. After the 1981 season in Visalia, I was traded to the Dodgers with my roommate Paul Voigt for an outfielder named Bobby Mitchell. Our performances while playing for Visalia against the Lodi Dodgers must have prompted the trade.

In 1981 Lodi was managed by Terry Collins, who was to be a big league manager for the Astros, the Angels, and the Mets. Either Terry put in a good word for me, or there was a powerful scout in attendance who liked what he saw when we played Lodi.

The 1982 camp with the Dodgers was an absolute blast! Big league camp was even more incredible, and the rooms were comparable to those in a fine hotel. You ate all you could eat, and it was better than dining out: grilled steaks, prime rib, salmon, chicken every way possible, and always pasta. During one dinner on the tablecloth-covered setting, Paul and I ate with the famous actor

Visalia pitcher Paul Voigt follows through in the Oaks' game against the Lodi Dodgers Monday night at Recreation Park.

Oaks top Lodi, 10-7
Madison snaps slump; Voigt wins 9th

By BRENT SWANSON
Times-Delta sports writer

The Visalia Oaks may have gained more than just a victory Monday night when they defeated the Lodi Dodgers, 10-7, in a California League baseball game at Recreation Park.

Scotti Madison, who has played a significant role in the Oaks' success this season, broke out of a slump by going 3-for-5 with two home runs and a single and driving in four runs.

"You can't believe how much pressure it takes off," Madison said. "When you're in a slump it's so much pressure. I was thinking instead of seeing the ball and reacting."

Manager Dick Phillips has called Madison a "worry wart" because the catcher "takes it home with him" when he has a bad game. But the skipper realizes Madison's importance to the team.

"He's got to get out of the habit of taking it home with him," Phillips said. "What happened tonight might be the best thing to happen to this club in awhile."

After Madison went 1-for-8 in Sunday's double-header with the Dodgers, Phillips said he would keep him out of action for a few days. He had Rick Austin penciled in to catch and Ray Stein as designated hitter before Monday's game, but pitcher Paul Voigt requested that Madison catch. It turned out to be the right move.

Madison was hitting .354 at the conclusion of the first half two weeks ago, but entered Monday's game hitting .337. He's currently hitting .342 and leads the team in homers with 15 and runs batted in with 70.

Madison cracked a three-run homer in Visalia's seven-run seventh inning.

Visalia's Kent Hrbek, who went 2-for-4 in the game, could have upped his average to .401 with a hit in his last at-bat, but went down on a called third strike on the inside corner. Hrbek, who has 23 hits in his last 46 at-bats, is hitting .397.

Lodi's Stu Pederson and Greg Smith had solo homers in the game. The Dodgers scored four times in the ninth to get back in the game, but Visalia reliever Lee Belanger ended the threat by striking out right-fielder Joe Rossi with two runners on to end the game.

Voigt, who gained his ninth win against four losses, took over the team lead in wins and is one of the league leaders in that department. He left with one out in the ninth after running into trouble.

"I got behind and they sat on the fastball," he said. "I had a seven run lead and figured I'd go at 'em."

Kevin Williams went 2-for-3 in the game and has six hits in his last eight at-bats.

(See box score in Scoreboard, page 6B)

OAKS NOTES: Visalia is idle today and opens a two game series in San Jose Wednesday night. The Oaks return home Friday night to open a series with the Fresno Giants. Eric Snider, who was released by the Giants earlier this season, joined the Oaks Monday and becomes their ninth pitcher. He is a right-handed fastball pitcher.

Tuesday, July 7, 1981, Visalia Times-Delta

Danny Kaye after Mr. Kaye asked to join us at our table. Dodgertown had all kinds of movie stars and singers joining us weekly, from country singer Barbara Mandrell to Belinda Carlisle, lead vocalist of the Go-Go's.

With the Dodgers, I spent most of my time catching in the bull-pen or catching batting practice. I probably averaged six to eight pitchers a day, every day of spring camp, and this lasted for nine more years. Each day I worked with determination and hustled like no one else did at Holman Stadium. The team scheduled defensive drills in the morning practices, and they asked for volunteers to get in the hot box or, as some refer to it, the "pickle." As the runner, your job was to make it back safely to a base while the defensive players tried to tag you out. I volunteered to be the runner every chance I got. I totally upset Dodgers veteran shortstop Bill Russell and the rookie newbie second baseman Steve Sax. They kept telling me to "chill, slow it down. This is just practice. You're making us look bad!"

While waiting for more catching assignments, I ran down balls in batting practice. Dusty Baker and Rick Monday might be stand-

Scotti and Paul Voigt.

ing side by side and catching whatever dropped within grenade range of them, but I was diving for balls all over the place. The chest of my uniform would be green with grass stains. In fact the Dodger equipment manager told me to stop getting my uniform so dirty at practice because he couldn't get the stains out.

I can remember Dusty Baker meeting my kids years later at a Braves game when Dusty managed the San Francisco Giants, and he told them, "Your dad practiced too hard. I have never seen anyone dive for balls like he did in practice. He was a Charlie Hustle." I definitely wanted to make sure I left all my effort on the field.

I thought about my years of playing baseball, and the practice it took to even get to Single A ball. One thing I could count on no matter where I played, there would be lot of repetition. You can guarantee that every year in spring training you practice the routine, the mundane, the boring, again and again. It is common knowledge in baseball that if you make the routine plays 90 percent of the time, you most likely will win 60 percent of your games. A team that wins 60 percent of the time will win its division and make the playoffs. If you win 60 percent of your playoff games, you take home the championship hardware. Thus, you have to do the routine, the mundane, the boring repeatedly until you perfect it. Then you go out the next day and do the exact thing again until the routine becomes so natural that you don't have to think about it. You start to react, and you know exactly what to do with the baseball when it comes to you in any and every situation.

The Dodgers would bring around their Hall of Fame coaches and players to mingle with the players at mealtimes and then dress them up in their Dodgers uniforms of past glory days and put them out on the field. Walter Alston, Sandy Koufax, and Roy Campanella were regulars on the Dodgertown fields. You could learn so much about the game just listening to them speak. I did everything I could to practice within earshot of their presence, for you never knew when a baseball memory would happen.

Roy Campanella broke into the league only one year later than

Feb/23/82

Dear "Ram Power",

Unbelievable! Absolutely fantastic! Words really can not describe this place as it is all first class. Besides the finest in baseball facilities second to none, it has the complete country club setting. The complex contains a four star dining room, two to a room and I mean plush, 2 olympic size pools, 12 tennis courts and 27 holes of golf. Since I came down here 2 days early, I have made use of all the complex.

Today was a most memorable day. Since the team does not have to report until tomorrow, the workouts are informal. Some of the guys are already here so I worked out with them. I hit for 40 minutes today, first from the left side off Joe Beckwith and then from the right side off Jerry Reuss. But guess who shagged for me and ran the balls down in the outfield? Dave Goltz (5 yrs for 3.5 million), Ron Cey & Sandy Koufax. Boy was I nervous at first! Especially, when about 100 people came up to watch as I hit. I ended up hitting about 15 over the fence and Cey walked up to me and said, "you are a pretty good hitter". In fact, I won a coke off Reuss when he challonged me to a half inning of game situation. I hit one over off him and won 1-0. Told him to credit it and I will go double or nothing. Reuss & Koufax laughed and said the kid is already popping off. HA!

    I will work hard and make a name for myself. Let me know what is going on up there. You got to delister.

           Best Wishes,
           Scott

P.S. WALt AlSTON is my Next door Neighbor!

Jackie Robinson, the man who broke the race barrier in baseball. "Campy," as they called him, was an All-Star player winning the Most Valuable Player award three times for the Brooklyn Dodgers. He hit with power and set records in baseball for RBIs and home runs. He also threw out 57 percent of the base runners that tried to steal off him, a league record even today. His nine-year career was cut short due to a car accident that left him in a wheelchair for life. The Dodgers took care of their heroes and kept Roy Campanella around as an honorary coach, and later on he worked in Dodgers community relations.

Now, we are on a field, and the Hall of Fame catcher is sitting in his wheelchair. I can think of no one I ever heard coach who was as passionate as he was. There he was, half a man in stature, but more than a man in the game of baseball. The love he had for baseball was still evident as he waved his hands above his disability, showing you the correct way to receive a pitch and block home plate. We catchers sat on our butts circling home plate, and Campy danced around in his wheelchair, bringing us knowledge and experience from the Negro Leagues and the Brooklyn Dodgers. From his wheelchair parked at home plate he said, "You don't think about what to do when the ball comes to you; you react. You think about it at practice; you react to it in the game. If you have to think about it during the game, you lose!" In other words, it takes repetition to be successful and perfect repetition again and again to be great.

To be a writer, a teacher, a lawyer, or a broom maker, you have to be willing to do the routine things. I don't know what that looks like in those professions, but in the world of an athlete, it is tireless days that are often lonely and way short of glamorous. It takes a lot of sentences to make a book; it takes a lot of ground balls to make a big league infielder; it takes a lot of swings to make a big league hitter; it takes a lot of pitches to make a big league pitcher. It takes a lot of doing the routine even to become a good Minor League player.

You cannot go through baseball or life wanting to be reasonably good at your profession and expect good results. Seeking to be just good will make you average, and it will not finish your book; it will not educate your students; it will not win your court case; and it will not make your broom the best in the store. For an athlete, you will not make the play!

Whatever becomes your pursuit in life, in order to achieve greatness you must be willing to do the little things with a willing spirit. To become excellent, you have to do the average again and again. Exceptional baseball players, especially those guys with the least amount of talent, love doing the little things. The passion for the game drives your love for it and helps you come early and stay late on the practice field. Most days, doing the little things will make the difference, will help you make the team, will help you reach your potential, and will help you win the championships.

I was willing to do the little things: fielding the mundane ground balls; hitting the relentless balls streaming from the pitching machine; catching the thrown balls from pitchers, hundreds and hundreds every day, thousands every week. This was what I lived for, and I had been doing this since the age of four. I loved practice, and if I were to make an impact on anyone in my career at spring training, it would become evident to all who were there that Scotti Madison would be the last one to leave the practice field every day. My ability might fail me, and someone else might have more tools, but I was determined that no one would outwork me. Of all the teams I played for, the Dodgers probably practiced the routine the best. Whatever work was given to me, I would do it, and I would love doing it. The routine in baseball was my lifeblood! It is great to be able to do something you love to do, and I loved to do baseball.

Every day at Dodgers spring practices, the coaches rotated the players to various fields to work on different aspects of the game. A whistle blew, and the coaches expected and demanded that the players sprint to each field to begin the next drill. I always toted my

Worth catching bag with me to each field. It not only secured all of my catching gear but usually consisted of a third base glove, a first base glove, an outfield glove, and at least three bats. My point is that it was real heavy, especially when I had to lug it over my shoulder and jog to the next field. Catchers carrying similar weight were not expected to sprint to the next station, but a steady trot was the rule of the day.

On one particular day, I glanced over my left shoulder to see the wiry Terry Collins (TC) approaching me. When I first met Terry a couple of weeks earlier, my first thought was, *This guy is too damn hyper for me.* For anyone who ever met me and recognized how hyper I was, this should give you a good indication about how high-strung TC appeared. In his early days, TC was aggressive, assertive, feisty, and above all else cocky!

One thing for sure, Terry Collins was loyal to his players, and he loved the Dodgers. His passion for the game may have rubbed some players wrong, but you knew right where he stood and I never found fault with a manager who was truthful and full of energy for the game. If Lasorda could have looked out past his plate of lasagna, he would have seen that Terry Collins would have been his best choice for third base coach. I would have driven through hell with my window down to please a guy like Collins, whom I always greatly admired because he was honest with me and appreciated the passion I had for the game.

Terry ran up alongside me and confidently boasted, "Madison, if I outrun you to the next field, everyone on the teams is going to have to run extra after practice."

The challenge was on, and we both took off at wide-open speed. Terry was built like the green clay humanoid Gumby, and all he was carrying was a Fungo bat. Of course, I was carrying my Worth catching bag filled with my armor.

Within about fifteen yards into the race, I realized Terry was about to get the best of me. I had to do some quick thinking to change the momentum and the outcome of the race. For some reason, I crazily slung my dark blue catcher's bag over my shoulder and hurled it in the direction of TC's next stride, right at his feet. It was the perfect toss, and a military sniper from one hundred yards away could not have catapulted TC in the air much higher.

TC landed all ass and elbows after doing what appeared to be a flip. His uniform had grass stains all over it, and he hated getting his uniform dirty, especially this particular way. He came up cussing and hollering at this Dodgers catcher, "What the hell are you doing?"

I was laughing all the way to the next dugout and hollering back, "I am winning this race! I am winning this race!"

Terry always appreciated my competitiveness from that day forward, and my spontaneous desire to win at all costs paid off when I played for TC in the 1983 season in San Antonio.

Even after all of this at the Dodgers spring camp, it would take a visit to Tommy Lasorda's office for me to completely understand the meaning of heading north and the trickle-down effect. Remember I had been hustling in Dodgers camp, and it was quite obvious to every player and coach how hard I worked. I never got any playing time, but I was a go-getter. Our lockers were next door to those of the big leaguers, and there were about twelve other nonroster players in camp with me during this particular Grapefruit League season.

Mark Cresse, who coached with the Dodgers from 1974 to 1998, was as fine a person as you could ever meet. He was always doing something to improve his lot. Once we saw him take a broken bat, hollow out the center with a wood tool, glue it on a home plate, and put a lampshade on it. He generated some good dollars with this unique baseball product. He was a solid man and the perfect bullpen catcher, a most likable fellow who has his own baseball camp today.

Mark was Tommy Lasorda's errand boy, and Tommy sent Mark to get me. His words were, "Tommy really wants to see you."

The best description of Tommy Lasorda would go something like this: his eyes appeared to bulge out of his head, and his cheeks were a first cousin to those of Santa Claus. He was the ultimate motivator. If Tommy ever got to talking, the only thing that might stop him was that everyone around him passed out from exhaustion upon hearing his stories. There was never a dull moment around him, and he was the ultimate storyteller. You left his presence feeling better about yourself or knowing that the Dodgers had a chance to win the pennant.

Well, I didn't know what to expect since the Grapefruit League for the big leaguers was ending in about five days. Looking into Tommy's office, I saw Joey Amalfitano, Danny Ozark, Ron Perranoski, and Manny Mota. Making a guest appearance was Sandy Koufax. It was quite the list of baseball legends, and I was at a loss for words. Each began to tell me, "Good job! Way to hustle! You play the game hard!"

Then Tommy dominated the praise among the group, saying, "Scotti Madison bleeds Dodger blue. No one plays like he does. If everyone came to the park every day and played as hard as he did, the Dodgers would win the World Series every year." Lasorda then asked the group to leave, stating, "I want to talk to Scotti alone." As the entire room emptied, every one of the guys patted me on the back and complimented my hustle.

At that point in time, I knew without a shadow of a doubt that I was going north with the big league club. Why else would they be saying these wonderful words of praise and affirmation? Here I was going to the big leagues, and I never even got a bat in a spring training game. I was viewing myself as the new Rudy Ruettiger of Major League baseball, finally being rewarded for dedication and determination, the foundational principles that my father and my uncle taught me about success. My breaking camp with the Dodgers would be the ultimate reward for my efforts.

Lasorda sang my praises for at least another five minutes, and then he said, "Hey, I need you to step over this way," which I confidently did. Lasorda opened a side door, which was the entrance into his personal bathroom. He stated, "If the great Dodger in the sky comes down to get you, Scotti Madison is who he is looking for!" While he continued to talk about the Dodger blue in the sky and how much I hustled, without missing a beat, he dropped his baseball britches and sat right smack on the toilet.

This was a first for me; I was not quite sure how to respond to this audacious move from Tommy. Think about it: he was continuing to tell me how great I was doing while he was perched only six to eight feet away.

Tommy was "doing his business," and I was trying to find a fresh air pocket of relief. Lasorda's diet was all starches, mostly Italian, and I was turning my head and gagging. Just before I got sick, I asked Lasorda if we could continue our conversation at a later date as I gasped and hurriedly reached for the doorknob.

Upon opening the door, I saw all the coaches who were present to begin the prank. They were standing outside the door, holding stopwatches to time how long I would stay in Tommy's bathroom with him. A huge laugh echoed among the coaches, and I was informed that I broke the record for longest time of being in Lasorda's office. (By the way, you may recall that Tommy did Slim-Fast commercials at one time.) Unfortunately for me, that occurred prior to this prank.

It was a joke that I will never forget, and it taught me a lesson about the trickle-down effect at spring camp. I didn't break camp with the Los Angeles Dodgers that spring, but I did break a record, which even to this day has not been surpassed.

Chapter 8
Good Old Tate High

B ack to the 1981 Twins camp. Herbie and I were still doing well, and I couldn't believe what I was hearing about these other players who were trickling down from Orlando. I was doing everything within my ability to get better every day at practice, and it just wasn't fair. I was the first to show up when the batting cages opened to work on hitting.

Let me rephrase that, batting cage. There was one cage, I repeat, one batting cage at the Twins Minor League complex. Thus, time was your adversary, and if you took thirteen swings, you had actually stolen an extra swing from someone else. I think you actually got twelve pitches, so if the ragged pitching machine acted up, you were encouraged to swing at everything that came your way. This was the philosophy of the Twins hitting instructor, Tony Oliva, a right fielder and designated hitter for the Twins.

Tony played his entire fifteen-year baseball career for the Minnesota Twins (1962–76). He was a left-handed hitter and had quite a career. He was Rookie of the Year, and he won three batting titles and was probably as good a hitter as there was in the show during his career. His career was hampered by knee injuries, forcing him to become a designated hitter during his final four years of baseball.

These same knee injuries forced him to bring a chair to the batting cage daily, and Tony coached while seated, perched right outside the screen as if he were the catcher. Occasionally, he would get up from his seat and walk into the cage to demonstrate proper plate coverage. He actually hit balls from the machine, showing you how easy it was to hit the outside pitch to the opposite field, still such a fluid swing at forty-three years of age. He could still smack the ball around, and hitting seemed easier to him than actually telling

someone how to hit. He was one of those coaches who had a difficult time communicating the message to a struggling hitter because
he was such a natural hitter.

He still had the perfect disposition and looked at everything
with a positive attitude. Tony was the shining example of the statement, "He has a smile on his face every time he talks."

Tony liked me due to my trip to Cuba, which we discussed several times. Oliva was born in Pinar del Rio, Cuba, and had not
retraced his steps back home after leaving. Every Cuban ballplayer
who made it to the United States dared not travel back to Cuba.
Fidel Castro's love for baseball just might keep them permanently
on the island discovered by Columbus in 1492! Tony's feeling of appreciation for the game and for the opportunity to become "somebody in baseball," as his dad so desired, is ever present to this day.

Back at the batting cage, Herbie and I did not get many extra
swings during camp. To improve our lot, we tried to convince Cal
Ermer that we had not hit yet. We hoped he would be forgetful, as
he often appeared to be, and then we would show up for a second
time to hit. Being a switch-hitter, I told Cal that Tony wanted me to
work on something on my left-handed swing, and then I told Tony
that Cal sent me back to get extra cuts on the right side of the plate.
It worked every time, and I wished I thought of that plan earlier
to escape some of the other mundane parts of practice. There was
nothing I enjoyed more than taking batting practice.

The main player who tried to steal extra swings in camp ended
up being my teammate and roommate in Visalia, Jim Weaver, affectionately known as "Dream." Jim played at Florida State and
was also on an All-America team with me. We played in Visalia
together in the summer of 1981, went our separate ways, and later
hooked back up with the Tigers organization some four years later.
Jim loved to hit so much that you had to run him out of a batting
cage. He was probably the best athlete this Vandy graduate had ever
played with to that point in time in baseball. Jim was strong, he
could throw, and he could run like the wind. He fell a distant third

Bo Jackson and Scotti.

in the "incredible athlete category," however, after I was later privileged to play with Kirk Gibson and Bo Jackson. (More on those two guys in my next book.)

One of the first games we played in the spring training of 1981 was against the Dodgers and Hall of Fame pitcher Don Sutton, who had traveled with the Dodgers B team to get some innings in on the mound. It was customary to see a star pitcher pitch in a B game in order to complete his training as he prepared for the regular season.

You might know Don for his exceptional Hall of Fame career, first as a player and currently as a broadcaster. In the Majors, he played a remarkable twenty-three years for the Los Angeles Dodgers, Houston Astros, Milwaukee Brewers, Oakland Athletics, and California Angels. A player like me with shoulder problems was astounded that a guy could play for twenty-three seasons, much less be a pitcher for that length of time. He won a total of 324 games, 58 of them shutouts and 5 of them one-hitters, and he is seventh on baseball's all-time strikeout list with 3,574 K's. His numbers warranted a Hall of Fame induction in 1998.

Yet what made Don special to me were the obstacles he had to overcome. For example, he holds the Major League record for number of consecutive losses to one team, having lost 13 straight games to the Chicago Cubs. He also holds the dubious distinction of being the player with the most at bats without a home run (1,354). He tells people the closest he ever got to a home run was a triple. Sutton holds another unlucky record: seven times in his career, he pitched nine scoreless innings, yet obtained a no-decision. Then there was his bout with kidney cancer in 2002, which he whipped.

You can tell a lot about the character of a man through the hardships that have come his way and how he overcame adversity. Don was a fighter and would not give in to anything, and such would be the case this particular day pitching against Herbie, Dream Weaver, and me.

Don Sutton graduated from J. M. Tate High School in Gonzalez/ Cantonment, Florida, thirteen years before I graduated from the same high school. After my graduation from Tate, the next Major Leaguer to come through Tate would be Jay Bell, who enjoyed much success in his thirteen-year career with two All-Star appearances, a Gold Glove Award, and a Silver Slugger Award. He is most recognized in baseball fame for scoring the winning run in Game 7 of the 2001 World Series for the Arizona Diamondbacks, skipping home in celebratory style from third base on Luis Gonzales's bloop single.

The next Tate High graduate in line for Major League fame was Travis Fryman, who also played thirteen seasons, won a Gold Glove Award and a Silver Slugger Award, and played in five All-Star games.

So there was some chemistry among all the Tate High boys, and this particular St. Patrick's Day in 1981, I wanted to talk with Don before the game. The last time we talked, I had called him when the Twins drafted me; I was seeking advice on contract suggestions some nine months earlier.

After some intel gathering, Don told me I was worth about $45,000, which encouraged this former Vandy player. Reality set in soon after that, and the chintzy Twins offered me $30,000 less than Don suggested.

Today, though, it was kind of cool that I, the newbie in the Twins camp, was standing near first base before the game, talking with the highly successful veteran, Don Sutton. Those watching our fraternizing could tell we knew each other from way back. Don asked how it was going, and I told him I felt that I had a good chance to make the Triple A squad, especially with a couple more good games.

Without my imposing on the star pitcher, Don volunteered to help me: "Hey, I'll give you a good pitch to hit today."

I told him I really appreciated it, and I would try to make the most of it.

Coming to the plate with men on first and second early in the game, I had my first at bat against the future Hall of Famer. There were two outs when I casually stared at Sutton on the mound. It wasn't apparent that Don wanted me to do well because he had this serious look on his face as he stared me down from the mound.

I worked the count to full, and it was then that I caught Don's eye. I could tell from his glance that he was going to lay a pitch right down the middle of the plate. It was almost as if he was calling out to everyone in the stadium, "Scotti, here comes a fastball right down Main Street!"

And sure enough Don threw a fat eighty-five-mile-per-hour fastball right down the middle of the plate. I laced it down the line and deep, and the only question was, Will it be fair or foul? Well, it was foul but not by much. You could hear a couple of ooohs and aaahs from a few fans scattered around the diamond.

Settling back into the batter's box, I just knew I was on the way to making the Triple A squad. Nothing changed; the pitch count was the same; Don was still my friend, so I anticipated another fastball delivered on a silver platter.

But Don didn't throw another fastball. He threw one of his patented, hands-of-a-clock, 12-to-6 curveballs, the one that drops off a tabletop and the pitch that would get him into the Hall of Fame.

Let me emphasize this point right now. It is extremely embarrassing to be hitting when you are 1,000 percent positive a fastball is coming, and you are actually being thrown the best curveball in the National League. In fact, I was lucky to catch my balance after my swing, or I would have fallen face-first in the batter's box. Totally embarrassed, I started walking across the field, and Don and I crossed paths near the first base line.

Still stunned by what happened, I asked, "Don, I thought you were going to give me a good pitch to hit. What happened?"

Don replied with a smile, "I did. I gave you a pitch to hit; you just need to learn to hit it fair!"

Chapter 9

"Nice Try!"

Another memorable St. Patrick's Day stands out in my memory several years in the future beyond this episode with Don Sutton. Yet before I got to that day, I had to enhance my bullpen skills using the art of negotiations. It would take place a year after my contract was purchased from the Dodgers, and I would be a Detroit Tiger. I loved spring training and especially enjoyed being a part of big league camp. There was nothing like going to the yard early in the morning and smelling the fresh-cut grass on the well-manicured ball fields.

For those who have had the privilege to tread on a professional baseball diamond, you can fully appreciate my sentiments that you must be in heaven when you are standing on the field. It gives you such a feeling of exhilaration when you step on a ball diamond that is perfectly prepared for a game. After an off-season of cold, inclement weather and constant practice indoors for three to four consecutive months, the feel of a baseball field in spring training is something you long for, and you will never forget the wonderful aroma of spring baseball. It provides you with a fragrance of hope and the feeling that it is time to start living again after the dead of winter.

When you combine the fresh spring air of rejuvenation with baseball fans excited that the rites of spring have finally arrived, you have the essence of spring training. Being the career Minor Leaguer that I was, the chance to participate in a spring training game in the big stadium was the best feeling I ever had in baseball. Just to sit on the bench and look at the stands filled with suntan-seeking baseball purists set you apart as special. To actually play in a game in front of the baseball faithful provided me with the ultimate feeling of satisfaction.

At spring training I really enjoyed sitting in the bullpen with the fans, who were all within a handshake of me. The majority of the time they respected my space and left me alone. Every now and then an overzealous fan asked for an autograph or possibly even a baseball. It was nothing to grant an autograph, and the atmosphere among the players was usually relaxed, so all would sign, even if it was against their nature.

I carried on conversations with a few fans during the game and worked the crowd to the bullpen's advantage. Souvenirs of all kinds are gathered up in earnest from loyal fans. The one jewel, the one prize, the ultimate souvenir was taking home a baseball. I learned to take a few extra baseballs with me and used the balls to barter for edible items served at the concession stand. There is something special about leaving a Major League game with a baseball in hand; it becomes a lifetime story of achievement. Walking home with a ball is certainly the crowning achievement for any kid who comes to the park and is no less important for grown-ups who wish they had kept playing. I have seen many a grown person sacrifice body and limb in an effort to catch a foul ball. So, a brand-new Major League baseball being offered up at the beginning of the baseball season contains incredible value. Imagine the story that is made up after receiving a baseball from the guys in the bullpen!

The very first time I sat in the bullpen for a spring game, I saw fans eating tasty-looking hot dogs, nachos, and other ballpark foods. There is something about a dog at the ballpark that intensifies the taste of a hot dog. Early on I recognized the value of a baseball to the average fan, and if players signed the ball, the value of legal bullpen tender went through the roof. Most fans along the foul lines where the players normally sat were not interested in a Scotti Madison autograph. No one had heard of me; yet the fact I was wearing a uniform and did not have to buy a ticket to get into the park set me apart from the fans in attendance. But if a baseball had a Madison signature and also a Willie Hernandez, Walt Terrell, Dan Petry, Frank Tanana, Jack Morris, Milt Wilcox, Mickey Mahler, Chuck Cary, or Randy O'Neal signature, I could pretty much ask for anything from the fan and get it.

Starting out small, I gave an unsigned baseball away for some hot dogs. I held a couple of baseballs in my hands and asked, "Hey, would anyone like to trade some hot dogs for a couple of American League baseballs?" There was always a taker or two, and teammates liked the extra treats I bartered for during the game. I had an unlimited supply of brand-new American League baseballs at my disposal, so my teammates in the bullpen never went hungry. Every player on "the take" usually walked away from the bullpen content, and any problems that arose were due to indigestion suffered while pitching in a spring game. Indulging in a bullpen treat always had serious ramifications for a relief pitcher who got called to the mound earlier than he anticipated.

Then I began to expand the enterprise and started asking for nonconsumable goods after only a few Grapefruit League games. This expansion of commerce first occurred when the Tigers took a road trip to play in Tampa. During this game, the location of the first base foul line was looking directly into the sun when facing the field. Even if you wore your baseball cap the entire time, the impact of the sun on your eyes created a headache within a few innings. Some of the other veterans traveling that day had anticipated the sun problem, and they took baseball glasses with them to the bullpen. These glasses were the flip glasses you see a lot of outfielders wear on a high sun day in baseball, mostly black in color and absolutely unfashionable.

Having no glasses in my possession, I started to develop a headache by the second inning. It was not one of those hunger headaches you sometimes get from not eating because I had already downed a hot dog from a baseball trade in the first inning. Thus, the culprit was the Florida sunshine pounding on my face, and it would be relentless for seven more innings if I did not come up with a solution.

I stood up, peered into the stands, and noticed several guys wearing stylish sunglasses. Being the entrepreneur at heart I was, I selected the best baseball out of the ball bag and borrowed a pen from the closest fan carrying a purse. I asked all the guys in the bullpen to sign "the pearl," a name that teammates often gave a baseball.

After obtaining seven or eight signatures from notable pitching stars, I began to sound like a vendor at the state fair hawking a chance at a six-foot teddy bear: "Hey, I have an official American League baseball right here in my hands with eight Major League signatures on it. Two of these guys are All-Stars! And me, I'm gonna be a Hall of Famer! Who wants to trade a pair of sunglasses for this autographed baseball?"

The guys on the bench in the bullpen looked at me and just laughed. For my part I wasn't quite sure where this full-fledged Madison Avenue marketing effort would end up. Were baseball fans willing to give up a pair of expensive sunglasses for a baseball with silly signatures on it? To my surprise, four fans raised their hands and almost fought for the opportunity to trade with me. I tried on each pair of their sunglasses trying to determine the perfect pair for my facial features and, most important, the glasses with the best UV radiation protection. I asked the cutest girl in the stands what pair looked best on me, and we decided on some Ray-Bans traded in by a Delta pilot.

Once the guys in the bullpen saw what transpired, they immediately asked me to get them a pair of glasses too. That day we walked away with six pairs of sunglasses, and six fans walked away with autographed baseballs signed by eight pitchers and a future Hall of Famer, or so they hoped. The last two pairs garnered were more difficult; they required a few extra autographs from players other than the Tiger relievers. So, I marched down to the third base dugout and asked Allan Trammell, Lou Whitaker, and Lance Parrish to please sign the baseballs for a needy and well-deserving fan.

By the time spring training was over, everyone in the bullpen had two to three pairs of stylish sunglasses, and I was set for Christmas with a variety of brands. Just another perk of being a big league ballplayer!

☎

On St. Patrick's Day, 1985, the Tigers were traveling to Vero Beach to play the Dodgers, and I planned to swap pelotas (Spanish slang word for baseballs) for some more sunglasses. Since I had been with the Dodgers two springs earlier, I remembered the visitors' bullpen was a direct hit for the sunshine that peppered Holman Stadium. Thus, I was prepared and had stashed a few extra balls away in my catching bag, anticipating a big take of glasses at the game.

On the bus, I was telling my Tigers teammates about St. Patrick's Day in Dodgertown: "The Dodgers spray paint the bases green, and all the players wear a green Dodgers baseball hat during the game." This strange occurrence on the diamond was due to the fact that Irishman Peter O'Malley owned the team, and it was a long-standing Los Angeles Dodgers' tradition honoring St. Patrick by bringing into play the color green.

The Tigers stepped off the bus to see Tigers fans everywhere. The nucleus of the 1984 World Championship team had traveled that day to Vero Beach, and the game would most likely set a record for attendance at Dodgertown. Because of the fame the Dodgers also carried with them annually, plenty of fans packed the small confines of Holman Stadium daily for a lesser opponent.

Now the World Champion Tigers were in town, so it was a festive atmosphere, to say the least. It felt like I was attending a Southeastern Conference football game due to all the hype outside the stadium. The Tigers dressed in traditional road garb: gray uniform with hints of blue and orange in the stripes and numbers. Nothing was happening out of the ordinary during batting practice, and my only predetermined role was to warm up the starting pitcher and everyone else who would pitch in the game that day.

I noticed over the right field fence and tree line that the Domino's Pizza jet had circled and was landing at the airport adjacent to Holman Stadium. I did not think it odd since Tom Monaghan was the owner and loved baseball as much as anyone in the stands. He was a great man, and I admired the story of how he started Domino's with a $75 down payment and then borrowed $900 to complete the payment for the first store. His partner was his brother, and eight months later his brother wanted out of the business. So, he traded his half of the pizza business to Tom for a used Volkswagen Beetle. Thirty-eight years later Mr. Monaghan would sell 93 percent of his company to Bain Capital for $1 billion.

The Tigers team completed batting practice, and each big league player walked into the visitors' dressing room to see what would be a surprise in his locker, a green Detroit Tigers' uniform. Dispersed through the lockers was the ultimate St. Patrick's Day baseball uniform complete with a solid green cap, green socks, a green belt, and green sleeves; the uniform itself had a green stripe down the leg, and the name *Detroit,* which spread across your chest, was green. Yet the dominant subject of discussion was the unique number on every player's jersey.

Every player has a favorite number on the field. The only reason he would not be wearing it is that another player, considered the star on the team, fancies the same number he likes. Today against the Dodgers, everybody would wear the same jersey number. Each player had the number 30 across his back, but no one could figure out why this particular number.

Some guys thought it must be a mistake for sure. The locker room was buzzing, and it took about fifteen minutes of discussion before a player finally figured out Mr. Monaghan's intentions. It wasn't a mistake; it was a stroke of genius. Tom Monaghan, philanthropist, American icon, and a true patriot to our country, owned

Domino's Pizza. The company's slogan in 1973 gave customers a guarantee that a Domino's Pizza would be delivered in thirty minutes or less upon placing an order or the pizza was free.

So, in this spring game with the Dodgers, the Tigers players would proudly wear the number 30 on their backs as the ultimate marketing opportunity advertising Mr. Monaghan's tag line, "30 minutes to deliver." It was totally remiss of us not recognizing that Mr. Monaghan had Irish blood in his heritage, so in his nature to win, he one-upped Peter O'Malley of the Dodgers.

The Dodgers wore only green ball caps with their usual uniforms, while the Tigers' entire uniforms were green. I know Lasorda didn't like the fact that we were the team everyone talked about that St. Patrick's Day when in years past the green ball caps worn by the Dodgers were enough to make them the talk of the town. But not today because Darrell Evans, Jack Morris, Alan Trammell, Lance Parrish, Larry Herndon, and the rest of the team walked out of that visitors' locker room wearing green Detroit Tigers' uniforms sporting the number 30.

Excited to be putting on this unique uniform, I figured I could acquire several pairs of sunglasses that day in the bullpen. The rest of the guys were laughing as they put on the uniforms, that is, all except two players, Chet Lemon and Lou Whitaker. These guys were star players, and they were also Jehovah's Witnesses. They explained to Tigers manager Sparky Anderson that their faith would not allow them to wear the green-colored uniforms; if they did so, they would be honoring St. Patrick.

Sparky told them, "No, you would be honoring Mr. Monaghan, who pays your salary!"

They staunchly refused to wear the St. Patrick's Day baseball uniforms, and Sparky told them to sit on the bus. Sparky then sent his first base coach, Dick "Trixie" Tracewski, to tell me I was starting in right field.

Sparky never talked to rookies and always had his assistant coaches do the talking for him to the younger players. One time

I was standing at the bathroom urinal, and to my right were Dick Tracewski in the middle stall and Sparky Anderson in the far right stall.

Sparky told Trixie, "Tell Scotti he is starting today!"

Trixie looked to his left and said to me, "You're starting today!"

I told Trixie, "Tell Sparky thanks!"

The news of a chance to play couldn't have been better. I wasn't just stealing a bat late in the game. Wow, I was getting a chance to start in a spring training game and against my former team, the Dodgers, which was the icing on the cake. I reasoned I could get sunglasses any day. I would make the most of this opportunity even if I was batting eighth and playing in right field.

Holman Stadium in 1985 was a quaint Florida spring training venue, with absolutely no shade to be found anywhere. The stadium was open, and the fans entered at the top and walked down some thirty steps to the bottom. Even the dugouts were open to the sun and fans, since there were neither sides nor a roof typical of a dugout. The only means of determining that it was a dugout was the one-foot wooden edge that sprang up from the ground and formed the foundation of the dugout. Benches were placed inside the wood-shaped rectangle, and it made grown men look like they were playing in a sand box.

The sun fell toward the third base stands, and everyone in attendance appeared to be wearing the color white or a shade of white. I think the Vero Beach Dodgers invented the whiteout for ball games. The combination of falling sun, white apparel, and a lot of retired folks with white hair made it quite difficult for players in the field to follow the flight of the ball as soon as it left the bat.

At the bottom half of the first inning, I sprinted out to my position of the day, right field. As I glanced toward home plate, the sun glared in my eyes. I really needed user-friendly sunglasses, but unfortunately, I had to wear those ugly outfield flip glasses that the rest of the team was wearing instead of a stylish pair I traded for during bullpen duty.

It was the first time I used a pair of baseball sunglasses, and I found them very bothersome to wear. The way the sunglasses sat underneath my cap, I could see the glasses in my peripheral vision when looking down at a ground ball. I kept trying to adjust them, flipping them down and up and down to try to figure out the best way to see out of them. I kept thinking, *I should have tried these on long before I started a game in the outfield!*

Jack Morris was on the mound that day for the Tigers, and his demeanor was not the most pleasant at times. I had never played with such a great athlete and pitcher who always seemed to be melancholy about something. Occasionally, there was a spark of laughter, but for the most part Jack seemed to be the most unhappy professional baseball player I ever played with. I tried to avoid him most of the time, and although Jack was cordial, he was not as nice to me as Parrish and Evans and Trammell. I even remember Roger Craig, the Tigers 1984 pitching coach, commenting to our Nashville Sounds team in 1985 how Jack was one of the most miserable people he ever coached in baseball. Roger perfected Jack's split finger fastball, and Jack was dominant on the 1984 World Championship team. He had the tools for success, but there just didn't appear to be much joy in Jack Morris's life on the field or in the locker room.

Morris toed the mound, and the third Dodgers hitter, Mike Marshall, stepped into the box with two outs in the bottom of the first. My former job as a batting practice catcher gave me a complete awareness of Marshall's hitting tendencies. I was sure that my intel on all the Dodgers hitters would pay off today, and I moved toward right center field, where Marshall hit the ball about 60 percent of the time.

While I was defensively positioning myself, I kept adjusting my glasses, hoping if the ball happened to come my way, I could see well enough to make the catch. It is amazing the power that people find in positive thoughts. It is just as amazing how powerful and destructive negative thoughts can be to the success of a ballplayer as well. Prior to the pitch to Marshall, I was second-guessing my experience, and my lifetime of playing baseball gave me no reassurance that I would catch a sun ball wearing these awful sunglasses. I was hoping the ball would not be hit to me.

Marshall hit the ball to right field, just as I was wishing that would not happen. It was worse than I imagined because he did not hit it to right center field where I placed myself. Marshall hit the baseball down the right field line, and I took off to try to catch the lazy fly ball tailing away from me. I must have flipped my glasses up and down twice before I got a bead on the ball. My sunglasses and ball cap by then had fallen off, and I was in a dead sprint to the right field corner in an all-out effort to make the play of the day.

I thought I had a chance to make the catch, based on my limited visibility looking into the sun, so I dove and extended outward as far as my body would allow in an effort to catch the sinking ball. I seriously miscalculated the flight of the ball, and when I landed on my belly, the baseball fell in front of me some twenty yards away from my outstretched glove hand. Lying on the ground, seeing the ball fall some two first downs away, I uttered a cuss word under my breath. That spring day, the fans saw what was probably the worst play on a fly ball in professional baseball history. The hustle and effort were certainly there on a picture-perfect dive, but the ball landed some three dives away and casually rolled to the right field corner. I hurriedly picked myself up, and I retrieved the ball by the foul pole and made an excellent throw to the cutoff man. Marshall ended up at third with a stand-up triple.

It was impossible to find a hole deep enough to hide in after that play. I know that some players fake injuries after a bonehead play, and I was hoping to have a slight heart attack. An ambulance transporting me off the field was the only way out of this butcher of a play. Everyone in the stands was laughing, and even my teammates were howling, sitting just a few yards away in the bullpen.

Jack Morris on the mound was not laughing, and he kept staring at me. I knew he was thinking, *That is the worst play on a fly*

ball I have ever seen in my life! Who is this guy? Jack seemed to stare in my direction for an eternity before he faced the next hitter. I was hoping that Marshall would not score on my blunder, and I was also hoping the Tigers would not send me back to the Dodgers and ask for their money back. Morris retired the next hitter, and Marshall was left stranded on third.

As I ran to the first base dugout with a sense of urgency, I felt like I was running in quicksand. I could hear the catcalls coming from all corners of the stadium; I had never been so embarrassed. It was another day in professional baseball when I provided free entertainment for everyone in attendance.

Near the bench, I looked up and saw Manager Sparky Anderson coming to greet me. Sparky, the baseball legend, was the first Tiger to say anything to me. He smiled and spoke to this star right fielder, "Nice try! You almost had that one!" That was the only time during the spring camp of 1985 that Sparky spoke to me. Other players may come and go, but I knew Sparky would never forget me!

Chapter 10

Stickers

M any times in the life of a baseball player you just feel like throwing in the towel. It is a hard life in the Minor Leagues, and you have to be mentally tougher than your situation. Camp was not conducive to fun; it was business, and you really had to rely on your mental toughness to make the most of each day. It is a mind game, so if you can keep your mind positive at all times by not allowing negative and destructive thoughts to enter your head, you just might make it!

The living conditions at Twins camp were close to state penitentiary living; we had four to a room, a community toilet, a community shower, and one pay phone for 150-plus players to use. Then there was the food that was horrible at best on a good day. Cell phones had not been invented, so you would have to wait hours to be able to use the phone. You could forget about hearing those comforting and supportive words from your family. I talked with my father only three times during the entire time of spring camp 1981.

To make matters worse, the Twins Minor League fields were atrocious, with holes in all of the batter's boxes and Florida sandspurs all over the outfield. The only comforting thought was that it was equally bad for everyone practicing there.

If there were ever a sticker you should hate, it would be the Florida sandspur known as *Cenchrus longispinus*. This devil of a plant likes sandy soil and can tolerate drought, cutting, fire, and most other nonchemical means of control. The Twins' fields were covered in sandy soil, especially in the outfield and batter's boxes. Thus, the outfields seemed to sprout forth with these spurs.

In appearance, the points are lightly barbed, really pointy, and quite painful at the touch. They are sneaky, so when you walk, they seem to leap onto your socks, cuffs, and shoelaces. Later when you undress, you find stickers all over your clothes. The sandspurs proliferated mostly in the outfield spots throughout the Twins' ball fields. Every day when we performed group calisthenics, we could count on picking three to four stickers out of our hands and twice that many off our uniforms. Guys picking these stickers off each other looked like monkeys grooming their caged mates in a zoo.

☎

If there was one thing to count on at spring camp, it was the requirement that extra work was the norm. To me, it was about paying your dues. I think I actually thrived off it! Even at times when there appeared to be a coach trying to get the best of me with excessive work, I would outlast the coach. I never asked to go in. The coach was the one who usually suggested I had enough!

No matter what organization you played for in baseball, there was always at least one coach in the Minor League camp who came to the yard daily with a chip on his shoulder. He was one of the "fallen ones," who had never reached their dreams or had not fulfilled their ambitions as Major League ballplayers. They usually were young coaches early in their careers, who had recently left the active playing ranks. Thus, the wounds of failure were still fresh in their minds, and they festered daily while coaching such promising talent. I felt as if these bitter souls almost resented the players who were following in their footsteps of chasing that elusive dream. These coaches sometimes pushed the young players to the edge, causing some awfully good talent to quit the game of baseball forever. I witnessed it several times when spring training mates walked away in frustration after an overzealous coach rubbed them wrong.

Despite my determined attitude to stick it out, no matter what, there were two times while coming through the ranks of the Minor Leagues that I strongly considered quitting. Both times, it could have been only God who provided me with the stamina and good fortune to finish the journey. Divine help often appeared to me through encouraging words offered through a loving and kind person, whose impeccable timing and appearance were more than coincidental.

I absolutely knew the coaching staff was trying to run me out of the game only one time in professional baseball. This particular episode began so innocently, turned badly in a morning practice, and finally ended with a laugh at first base some four years into the future. This impactful moment happened in the fall of 1981, in October to be exact, when the Twins Instructional League almost became my last league in baseball.

Each Major League team invited its top prospects to take part in Instructional League for additional instruction. The daily routine consisted of practice in the mornings, with special attention and focus directed at those areas of the game that were keeping you from advancing to the next level. After the morning work, you took a break for lunch, which usually consisted of soup, some crackers, some fruit like an orange or banana, and maybe a cold, stale sandwich. Most of the time the oranges were the first to go, since the Latinos viewed oranges like southerners view fried chicken.

You entered the lunch hour covered in sweat from a hard morning workout. Even in the fall, Florida is extremely humid, and you would be soaked with perspiration all the way down to your socks. Changing into dry underclothes seemed like such a pleasure during the day, so you would change out your underwear and T-shirt for a dry set for the afternoon game. Your socks were always wet and never came off because Big Fella Hattaway issued only one pair of socks in the morning at Twins camp. It was customary to steal a pair and double them up because one sock most likely had a hole in it, so wearing two pairs was the status quo. You usually finished the afternoon games by 4:00 p.m. at the latest, quickly dressed in street clothes, and were running out of the locker room for the beach by 4:30 p.m.

Fall Instructional League 1981 was loaded with talented players such as Tim Laudner, Gary Gaetti, Randy Bush, and Jeff Reed. I have to include my roommates Jim Weaver, Lee Belanger, and Tim Teufel in the talent pool. Tim and I knew each other from the Cape Cod Summer League of 1979, both playing on the Cape in our junior years in college. We later became roommates in Orlando the summer season of 1980. Tim played at Clemson and was also an All-American. We both had been drafted a total of three times before we finally signed with the Twins. Tim was playing extremely well and fast-tracking to the big leagues. He would soon enjoy ten years in the show with the Twins, the Mets, and the Padres.

The daily schedule allowed for too much free time in the afternoons and evenings after baseball, at least for me. Most players lived within slingshot range of the beach, which made it conducive to entertaining guests daily after practice. My buddies and I trolled the shoreline for prospects and invited the local talent back to our beach dwelling for afternoon happy hours. The bait usually consisted of young well-conditioned athletes, alcohol, and lots of laughs. It was a lifestyle promoting destructive behavior.

One time I brought back a new friend and ended up riding her bicycle on top of our roof. My buddies never figured out how I got the bicycle on the roof and were amazed I didn't ride right off the top. I never knew how I got up there, either, or how the bicycle ended up with two flat tires! The last thing I remember was taking her bicycle out of the trunk, tossing it on the lawn, and speeding away while her boyfriend was chasing my car.

For the most part, daily meals were meager and nonnutritious. But every other Friday, each of us pocketed $300 cash and instantly became Mississippi Saturday night rich for several days. The Twins paid us only a total of $600-a-month cash salary to play in Clearwater.

That was just not enough income for me; after all, I reasoned, I was a Vanderbilt graduate and had aspirations of better pay. I was already working in the insurance business with American Family Life Assurance Company (Aflac) in Nashville during the off-seasons. So, I was accustomed to working outside of baseball, and

I wanted to find extra work to gain other work experience in a new field. I also realized the bicycle trip on the roof was a wake-up call, and I needed to make better decisions before I killed myself or some jealous boyfriend beat me up. My desire to find work away from the field in the Instructional League soon created a disastrous situation for me with the Twins coaches.

☎

After practice one hot Florida day, two weeks into the season, I left practice and interviewed with the Brown Derby Restaurant on Roosevelt Boulevard in Clearwater. I immediately got the job as the host. I asked about becoming a bartender, but after I told them about my Vanderbilt degree, they wanted me in their management training program. I agreed just to get the job, knowing full well that fall baseball was over in two months, and more than likely I was heading back to Nashville.

The hours were great at the Brown Derby, and it was a good escape from my day job and any self-destructive opportunities I might otherwise seek. The restaurant schedule consisted of arriving at work in a shirt and tie by 5:00 p.m., and I worked until around 10:00. I looked at it as a way to stay out of trouble, leave the beach scene, and also make extra money. I also soon learned that the waitresses were nice and accommodating to a professional baseball player. It would be the perfect job for me, coinciding with day baseball; that is, until the day my coaches showed up to the restaurant and needed a table to dine.

I really did not want the coaches to know I had a night job in the food and beverage industry. If they had asked me directly, I would have told them the truth about the night employment. I think they would rather that I drank beer in the afternoon with my teammates, raised a little hell, and had just been a "guy's guy" ballplayer. That seemed to be status quo for a lot of players and was certainly my rally cry until God shook me after my rooftop experience.

I remember in the movie *An Officer and a Gentleman*, Gunnery

Sergeant Louis Gossett Jr. was hammering on the rebellious Richard Gere. Gere took advantage of his fellow soldiers, and Gossett was trying to break him with excessive punishment. Gossett kept telling him to quit and finally said, "Why don't you quit?" Gossett relinquished and backed off only after Gere responded, "I got nowhere else to go!" I wonder if every Major League organization wanted a similar situation for its young prospects? When you have "nowhere else to go," you are in a highly motivated place in life. Desperate players produce better results. It certainly works well for the Latin ballplayers, since their only avenue leading out of poverty is through baseball. When you have a night job, I guess it appears to coaches that you're not highly motivated to play baseball. In their eyes, I had somewhere else to go.

What might have been hard for the Twins coaches to understand was that the job as a host had no detrimental impact on my love for the game and did not lessen my intensity on the field. I still gave it my all every day, and I always would. I just wanted options in life.

During fall Instructional League, Twins pitching coach Jim Shellenback (Shelley) always saw a common laborer outside the bus when we traveled across town to play another organization. Most of the time the man we could see through the window held a construction job, obvious from his hard hat.

Shelley yelled through the bus, "Hey, guys, see that guy over there? He is in the Lunch Box League, and if you don't make it in baseball, there you go. There is no future. It's a dead end. If you don't make it in baseball, next stop, Lunch Box League!"

The coaches might have resented the fact that I had something to fall back on if baseball didn't pan out. I think they wanted baseball to be "all or nothing" for every player with respect to a career. After all, that's how it appeared to be for many of them. Most coaches did not have a college degree, and once their dreams of playing professional baseball were stone dead, they turned to coaching. There appeared to be no backup plan for many in the game after playing the game. Every player eventually goes the way of the game, and you have to give it up one day. Was their coaching profession out of choice, or was it out of necessity?

I didn't want coaching baseball to be my only option after I quit playing. If I were to become a coach in professional baseball, it would be because it was my first love, not because it was the only profession available by default. There may have been other players with degrees, but I knew of only two other teammates with college degrees while I played: Orel Hershiser and Paul Voigt. The big difference between 98 percent of the guys playing in the Minor Leagues and these guys was that they had options. I would not be a slave to baseball; I played because I loved it! I wondered what was the greater motivator: you play the game because you have nowhere else to go, or you play something because you truly love it?

☎

Back to the restaurant. The afternoon game in fall ball went into extra innings, and I was late getting out of the park. After I fled the Twins clubhouse, I put on my yellow tie in the car before walking into the restaurant. I was only there for about an hour when I looked through the front glass door and groaned: "Oh no! It can't be!"

The hostess working with me asked what was wrong. It was too late to respond as Manager Tom Kelly (TK), and Coaches Jim Shellenback (Shelley), Rick Stelmaszek (Stelly), and Tony Oliva walked up to the hostess desk.

As I stood at the counter, the coaching group had this puzzled look on their faces while gazing at me. I looked directly at TK and, with an uncomfortable smile, calmly asked my manager, "Would you like a booth or a table?"

Without any expression or emotion coming from his face, an eternity seemed to pass before TK responded, "A booth!"

My heart sank, and a lump developed in my throat as I sat them down in a booth. I left them with a final, "I hope you enjoy your meal."

After dining, the coaches left without saying a word to me. At the restaurant, the exchange was uneventful, but I had this gut feeling that practice was going to take a turn for the worse the following day. And boy, was I right about that!

As usual, I was one of the first guys to arrive at the yard. I walked onto the field to practice and heard TK holler out for me to go and see Stelly. I walked over to Rick Stelmaszek, and the juice from his chaw was already dripping out of his mouth at 9:30 a.m. His right hand held his weapon of choice, a batting Fungo.

After retiring as a player-coach in 1978, Rick Stelmaszek remained as the manager of the Wisconsin Rapids through 1980. He was named Midwest League Manager of the Year in 1980 after leading his team to a 77–64 record. Following the season, he joined the Twins' Major League coaching staff under first Johnny Goryl and then Billy Gardner. As of 2012, Stelly observed his thirty-second consecutive season on the Twins' coaching staff and was third on the all-time tenure list of coaches, trailing only Nick Altrock and Manny Mota.

This particular day he looked quite focused; he looked as if he were about to inflict some pain. He was on a mission when he growled, "Are you ready to block some balls?" His speech was barely understandable, and the words were fighting through the dark tobacco juice creeping from the corner of his mouth and down his chin.

I had participated in many catching drills to block balls over the years, and I actually liked it. I thought blocking a wild pitch from an errant throw from the mound was a critical part of the game, so a little extra work to enhance this skill was just fine with me. I was not mentally prepared for what was about to occur, however, for this would soon become one of the most agonizing days of my life in the game of baseball.

Stelly and I walked to the batting cages and climbed through the netting together. I laid my catching gear to the side when Stelly told me to "strap 'em on and get behind the plate." I strapped on my gear, and my back was turned as I walked away from Stelly and toward home plate at the far end of the cage.

Like a dishonorable gunslinger in a pistol duel, my adversary soon fired the first shot my way before I barely turned my head. As soon as I squatted in a game-ready position, Stelly started firing baseballs rapidly in my direction off his Fungo bat. A Fungo is a special bat used for hitting fly balls or ground balls during warm-ups, thinner than a bat a hitter would take to the plate. It was designed to generate more bat speed hitting balls you toss up to yourself. In other words, you can hit a ball extremely hard with it, far enough to carry a ball from home plate to the fence in the outfield. The confines of a batting cage are extremely close: only sixty feet, six inches from the mound to home plate. Stelly was standing a good ten feet in front of the mound, which shortened the distance even more.

He rocketed balls as hard as he could hit them, and he told me to block them all. Balls were ricocheting off my forearms, my inner thighs, my neck, and my throwing hand, all areas unprotected with flesh exposed. I must have blocked or attempted to block some thirty to forty balls.

Finally, I had enough, stood up, and told Stelly, "I want to go to the bathroom."

Stelly moved out of the way and, in a firm tone, told me, "You're not finished yet!"

I scuffed past the Twins coach and on to the locker room. He was still in my personal space when the juice from his tobacco splattered on my jersey as he told me to hurry up!

This former Vanderbilt All-American was beat down; my spirit to play baseball had disappeared! I was walking into the locker room ready to go home. I was quitting! I was giving up on the dream to play in the Major Leagues. I guess that was why it was so easy for me to identify with Paul Newman in the movie *Cool Hand Luke*. There was Paul Newman in the middle of the yard digging a ditch, putting the dirt on the ground, filling the hole back up, and then forced to repeat the process again and again. During the process, they beat him down physically and mentally. Prior to his castigation, Newman had such a spirit for living, yet at a heightened level of punishment, his zeal for living was taken away, and Newman gave up. I had enough too! That day, I was right there in the prison yard with Paul Newman, and Cool Hand Luke was walking away from baseball forever.

I fled to the safety of the locker room and went directly to my locker. There in my home away from home for the past three weeks I began to take off the catching gear, stripping down to just my underwear and undershirt. Everything was piled up on the floor in a heap around my feet, and just like a cherry on top of an ice-cream sundae, my catcher's mitt created the pinnacle for the mountain of apparel.

I began to sob, for the pressure of the moment was unbearable, and reality had set in; I was giving up on a dream for the first time in my life. I wept deeply to the core of my soul for God to help me and to take me out of the damaging situation; the degrading episode in the batting cage had broken my spirit.

☎

It wasn't long, maybe a matter of seconds after my heartfelt plea to God, when an older man walked through the door of the locker room. It was Bob Smith; he and Rip Kirby were the leaders of Baseball Chapel at Jack Russell Stadium that fall. Yet to me, Bob was not a man but a God-sent angel that day. His timing was more than coincidental.

To understand and fully appreciate the situation, you have to know the evangelical dynamics occurring in camp that fall and throughout all Minor League baseball. There was a God movement taking place, and Baseball Chapel was making its way throughout the Minor Leagues. Arguably, the Minor Leaguers needed it more than the big league players. Younger players, many away from home for the very first time with cash in hand for the first time, were turning to alcohol, drugs, and random sex to combat loneliness. When you combine these destructive vices with the pressure that every Minor League player feels, recognizing his chances of making it to the Major Leagues were a slim 4 to 5 percent, Baseball Chapel, in my eyes, helped save many in the game.

In 1979 Rip Kirby of Knoxville, Tennessee, began coordinating a Baseball Chapel for the Minor Leagues, often meeting in the most remote places of a ballpark. Within five years, Kirby claimed that they had organized some 140 pastors and laymen volunteering to lead nondenominational services in some 150 cities for ballplayers. What a man for God and what a movement!

We were at the beginning of this movement in the fall of 1981, and either Rip Kirby or Bob Smith every Sunday invited the players of both teams to sit in the grandstands of Jack Russell Stadium in Clearwater to help escape life's pressures and face their problems head-on. The story would be surrounded by a Bible scripture, and for most of us, it was the only lesson about love and hope we would hear for the entire week. We were young men, most of us lost in our way, very lonely, missing the comfort of our family. The security of innocent past lives was long gone. Worst of all, we felt we were invincible! That becomes the mind-set of professional athletes when we start thinking we are important.

Rip and Bob were trying to assist young players who were facing a difficult time, and they were providing a valuable service to professional baseball. They were hoping to equip young men to handle the tough issues that our world throws at us every day.

I don't know how the reception was for Jesus in other locker rooms at that moment in time, but I can attest to the fact that the Twins organization expressed reservations about God having access to the players. In the life of a professional baseball player, every day is the same, so Sunday morning means just another day at the ballpark.

Baseball Chapel was a player's only chance to attend anything resembling a church service. Those attempting to attend Baseball Chapel recognized we weren't perfect and we didn't have to be. We just needed to be progressing in the right direction, and attending

Chapel every Sunday was certainly a step in the right direction to get our lives in order.

Instructional League demanded that you do some hard self-evaluation of your game and then agree to work on the areas that were lacking. It is difficult as a player to admit you have an imperfection on the field and then agree to spend two and a half hard months practicing on that particular baseball flaw. But you must improve in the area that is ultimately hindering your chances to become the type of ballplayer required to play in the big leagues. Well, we all had character flaws, too, and those imperfections were keeping us from being the kind of men that God expected us to become.

Bob Smith was about sixty-five years old, balding white on his head, and possessed the demeanor of a man filled with peace and purpose. Bob had exercised much patience with Tom Kelly, the head coach at Instructional League, doing what he could to meet with Twins players during the day. Some of our players were starting to realize there was more to life than baseball and more to life than this secular world. At the time, TK, probably at the urging of Minor League Director George Brophy, provided Bob and Baseball Chapel limited access to TK's players. Yet Rip and Bob were steadfast and made the most of it every Sunday for a brief, encouraging service held in the grandstand.

Mr. George Brophy terminated one Baseball Chapel service while it was in progress. It was a beautiful early November day in Clearwater, and the attendance was high in our Chapel service with players from both teams sitting side by side in the stands. Probably two-thirds of the Twins team were in attendance, and everyone was in a good mood, since there were just two games left in our fall Instructional ball season. Rip was in the middle of his lesson when the players noticed the Minor League Director, Mr. George Brophy, walking up the steps toward our makeshift service.

Mr. Brophy was about to drop a bombshell in the middle of our gathering. Brophy addressed the team and Rip quite sharply: "Men, I want you to hurry up with your meeting and get back to baseball.

Right now we are in first place in this league, and we want to win this thing. You need to end this talk and start concentrating on our game today!"

As Brophy walked away, we were in shock, and Rip politely told us, "I am sorry. We need to stop this service. No matter how we feel, we need to respect their wishes, even as wrong as we think it might be. Maybe we could pray for Mr. Brophy!"

None of the players was a seasoned Christian, and it was hard for us to take Brophy's insensitive demand with the proper outlook that a mature, godly man should have. I know none of us prayed for Mr. Brophy that day. After all, this was the same man who controlled the purse strings of our financial existence, so there was plenty of resentment toward Brophy already festering in each player's mind. I often wondered when Mr. Brophy was battling cancer later in life: Did he ever go back to that moment in time in Clearwater, Florida, and wish he had a do-over? We all could use do-overs!

So you can see, we sensed there was considerable friction within the organization about the idea of Jesus having access to the lock- er room. Fortunately, enough players who were believers attended Baseball Chapel regularly to create a feeling within Tom Kelly of a reluctant acceptance. Kind of like the "don't ask, don't tell policy," except this was the "don't ask, don't tell me about it" course of action.

This particular day at Twins fall camp, God won out because Bob, either through a fortuitous glance at the batting cage or a di- vine intuition that something was wrong, entered the locker room and walked up to me and my pile of clothes with words of comfort. He said, "Son, I know it's hard right now for you and you feel like quitting, but God loves you, and he is with you even in the darkest times. It is dark right now for you, but don't you allow any man to steal your dreams that God is a part of. Put your uniform back on, and don't quit because of what a man does to you."

Immediately a peace came over me.

Bob gave me a hug, and I began to put my sweat-drenched uni- form back on my battered body. About the same time I buckled my belt and placed my hat atop my head, TK walked into the locker room.

TK also sensed that I was quitting based on what he witnessed in the batting cage, and he would have liked nothing more than to have caught me out of uniform. I often wonder what it would have been like if just TK and I were in the locker room that morning. I fear he would have gotten the best of me, and I would have gone home that day, never playing a game in the Major Leagues.

TK asked, "What are you doing?"

I told TK that I had gone to the bathroom, and TK adamantly told me to get back out there to practice. I know Tom Kelly wanted to say more to my face that Instructional League morning, but my protector, my guardian angel, Bob Smith, was standing between failure and me.

TK quietly allowed this catcher to walk back out on the field. I never climbed back into that batting cage again, at least never again for a drop zone of well-aimed baseballs off Rick Stelmaszek's Fungo bat.

☎

I told you earlier that this story ended with a laugh at first base some four years later, and you may find that hard to believe, but it did. By then, I was playing with the Royals, and we traveled to play the Twins in a spring training B game. All that means is that you play a game on a practice field instead of the main stadium, where paying fans usually see their heroes perform. The Royals and the Twins were playing on a backfield adjacent to the big stadium, and there were still some stars playing that day for both sides.

I was playing first base for the Royals, and Tom Kelly, who was now the Twins big league manager, was coaching first base. It was not odd to see TK coach first in spring training. I think he liked being on the field and talking to the other players, as well as his own players who happened upon first. If you ever got on TK's good side, you found a guy who had a real dry sense of humor. He was a very likable guy, and even I have laughed many times at some of his comments while under his tutelage.

Tim Laudner had just picked up a hit and was standing at first. His past was checkered as a teammate with me going all the way back to playing together in Kenai, Alaska, and last playing in the Twins Instructional League. Thus, both TK and Laudner were familiar with my day of hell in the cage as well as my former job at the Brown Derby Restaurant.

With Laudner and me standing on first base prior to the pitch, TK standing beside us told Laudner, "Hey, I want you to get a big lead and get picked off right here." This was totally out of the ordinary for a manager to tell his player to purposely make an out.

Tim looked at TK in disbelief and replied, "What . . . what are you talking about? You want me to get picked off? Why would you want me to do that?"

Tim and I just stared at TK, our heads facing away from the field.

With a straight look on his face, TK said, "We got to hurry and end this game. Scotti has to be at the Brown Derby Restaurant to work the lunch crowd today."

All three of us began to laugh so hard that the first base umpire had to call time-out. There was a delay in the game due to the cackling at TK's remarks and the element of truth that surrounded his comment. Both dugouts were looking our way, wondering what could have possibly been so funny.

I knew it was TK's way of apologizing; the hard feelings were over now. It was as if that moment in time with Rick Stelmaszek in the batting cage never occurred. TK and I said hello every time we were on the field together from that day forth. Rick Stelmaszek is a friend! Time and grace really do help heal the unpleasantries that occur in life!

Chapter 11

The Bear

One other time I was prepared to walk away from the game, only to have a man with heart gather me back up, keep me focused, and set me on course for a cup of coffee in the Major Leagues. It began with my tenure with the Dodgers, starting first at spring training in 1983. My second year with the Dodgers, I would be invited to big league camp as a nonroster player. I was steadily recovering from shoulder problems after determining a plan of action working with the team doctors, trainers, and physical trainers with the Dodgers.

The spring prior to 1983, I had met with Dr. Frank Jobe numerous times to determine the status of my shoulder. I had thrown footballs and baseballs on a regular basis, from high school through college, without the first bit of knowledge on individual shoulder recovery exercises. That type of rehabilitation exercise had yet to be determined, much less attempted. Dr. Jobe, besides performing the Tommy John surgery, with the assistance of the Dodgers staff devised the first known shoulder exercises that are still used today. I started the recovery exercises in the spring of 1982, and my shoulder had grown much stronger and was pain free.

Then almost overnight it started getting worse, even though I was religiously doing my arm exercises. Halfway through the season in San Antonio, my shoulder started affecting my play, and I had to sit out some games due to pain. Since I couldn't throw without pain, I was mentally frustrated, and if you are not right in the head, you can't hit.

Nothing was more frustrating to me than missing games because of an injury. An even worse feeling was that I was doing everything I thought that had been correctly prescribed for me at the time, by assumedly the best arm doctor in the world, Dr. Frank Jobe. I was going to my trainer, Charlie Strasser, on a daily basis, and we just could not figure out why my shoulder continued to bother me.

Charlie (Chuck) came to the Dodgers by way of the Cleveland Cavaliers and was extremely knowledgeable in kinesiology, light-years ahead of my former trainers for the Twins. Charlie was a great guy and a friend of mine; I actually lived with Charlie, sleeping in his garage, for part of the season.

Charlie often told the story of the time he and his wife were asleep, and they heard a bear bellowing outside their bedroom window just west of suburban San Antonio. He kept hearing this huge roar and a deep grumbling sound. "Aaaaaarrrrrhhhhhh!" Charlie considered dialing 911. Instead he went outside with a baseball bat to see if he could run the bear off.

With a flashlight in one hand and a Louisville Slugger in another, Charlie nervously turned the corner to spotlight the culprit and found him with the trashcan open. In actuality, it was me heaving the remains of a decadent night of too much fun.

Charlie spoke with some relief, "Damn, I kept hearing this bear out my window growling. We almost called 911! I didn't know it was you throwing up."

I just told him, "I'm okay. I'm okay," as Charlie laughed all the way back to bed.

Back to the shoulder. Charlie and I couldn't figure what was causing my shoulder to hurt that season, even after a year of performing arm exercises. I finally got some relief and the answers to my arm problems in the spring of 1983, just in time to save my career.

Dr. Jobe had correctly prescribed the proper arm exercises for the rotator cuff injuries, but Jobe and the Dodger training staff had misdiagnosed the correct amount of weight to use. I started out on exercises with a one-inch roll of tape and progressed to exercising with a ten-pound dumbbell. Everyone rehabbing the rotator cuff slowly improved only to suddenly get worse overnight. They finally figured out that the maximum weight to use was three pounds. The secret to a stronger shoulder was less weight and more repetitions. I had been using too much weight for an entire season.

Thus, I began shoulder recovery one more time in spring training of 1983. With a bum arm, I faced the possibility of not making a team. At that point I was just catching, so what team needs a catcher who can't throw to second base or even to the pitcher without pain?

I was considering my options with the Dodgers. It was my third spring training, so I was becoming accustomed to the trickle-down effect, and I was counting released catchers daily as the list was becoming shorter and camp was soon to break. Even though I had hit .342 in Visalia in 1981, I was coming off a year hitting only .235 in San Antonio with a short stint of eleven games played in Albuquerque.

The only Dodgers manager to see me play well was Terry Collins, who had not yet made it to Double A. Fortuitously for me, the Albuquerque manager Del Crandall had taken a liking to me. Boy, did Del have a great career as a player winning four of the first five Gold Gloves ever given to a catcher and having eleven All-Star appearances in sixteen seasons. Then Del managed two big league clubs, the Milwaukee Brewers and the Seattle Mariners. Now, he was with the Triple A Dodgers farm club, and Del would be highly successful in Albuquerque. He was the one guy in camp who believed in me as a catcher; I was most fortunate to be playing for Del. I don't think Del ever believed I had big league stuff, but he knew I had a big league heart. He eventually taught me a lot about calling a game and setting up hitters. I was a sponge for baseball knowledge, and Del soon recognized my passion for the game. I looked at him as a father figure, which was why it hurt so profoundly the day Del quit believing in me.

☎

At the time, I was playing fairly well for the Dukes, hitting .292 with two home runs and twelve runs batted in after only twenty-three games in the lineup. My shoulder was getting better, and Del kept preaching to the team and me: "My job is to get you to the big leagues, and I want to see you succeed, so I am going to let you play in situations to give you a chance to succeed." And to that point in time, that was pretty much true. I was platooning with Dave Sax, the brother of Dodgers second baseman Steve Sax, and Jack Fimple.

Jack had come over from Cleveland in a trade, and his baseball strength was defense. He had a strong arm, and at the time, it was better than mine. I liked Jack, and we roomed together some on the road, which does not happen much when two players play the same position.

A funny story about Jack occurred in the Major Leagues when he was promoted to play for the Dodgers in the September call-up. Three other players were also called up and arrived in the big leagues together. But Jack Fimple was missing. Lasorda was upset and wanted to know why Fimple wasn't on the plane with the other three players.

The next day Jack arrived and handed Lasorda a letter. It was a written excuse from a taxi cab driver. The letter stated that the cab had a flat tire, and that was why Jack missed the plane. Can you believe a ballplayer handing his manager an excused absence from a taxi driver?

☎

Before I get back to Del Crandall, allow me one more story about Jack and me. It happened in Las Vegas in 1983, their first year to have the Triple A Stars baseball team. After a game, the two road roommates decided to go to Caesar's Palace (or we might have been staying there). Anyway, the casino was packed since the Jerry Lewis Muscular Dystrophy Association Telethon was taking place on the premises, and we were perched above the main casino floor.

From our vantage point we were pointing out all the TV stars to each other, catching Telly Savalas's attention once.

We kept noticing the ladies working the room, and they finally confronted us Albuquerque players. The ladies asked, "Would you two gentlemen like some company?" Both Jack and I said, "No thank you, but if you would like to stand here and have a drink with us, we are okay with that."

The ladies said, "We are too busy for that. What do ya'll do for a living?"

Jack responded, "We squat for a living!" They had no idea that meant both of us were catchers, and they didn't believe us when we told them we were in town to play against the Las Vegas Stars. The girls told us they were schoolteachers, and we didn't believe them either.

They actually stayed and chatted two drinks' worth, and we had some laughs. Sadly, we determined they were Midwest farmers' daughters who had gone astray. We certainly never took them up on their proposition, but we invited the gals to come to the park the next night; we would leave them guest passes at the gate.

The next day we left them some tickets, not really expecting the girls to show up. I will never forget the sight when both of us catchers were standing in front of the visitors' dugout and playing catch before the game. The entire team heard, "Hey, Jack, hey, Scotti, we're here!"

We looked up to see five women coming down the stairwell heading to the end of the dugout. Without a doubt you could tell they were not schoolteachers, and Jack and I had nowhere to hide as the women kept hollering at us, catching everyone's attention.

Every man in the stands was giving the trendy-dressed girls "the buck look." You know, the kind of look a big whitetail buck gives a hot doe when she walks into a field of clover. The buck stops whatever he is doing, he raises his head up, lust comes over him, and he stares directly at the female deer, checking her up and down with just his eye movements. Every other buck in the vicinity senses a doe has entered the field, and all the male deer gawk simultaneously at the lady looking in the same direction with the same intensity; neck is stiff, shoulders pushed back, eyes rapidly checking out the possibilities. There is no expression on the face; the wandering eyes tell it all! The buck look stare occurred throughout the entire stadium since the ladies were dressed like Julia Roberts in *Pretty Woman*.

Dukes manager Del Crandall glanced at all five women and then stared at both of us catchers and said, "I am giving both of you a $50 fine for missing curfew last night." We never missed curfew, but rather than argue with Del, we paid the $50 and laughed a long time at the expression on Del's face when he first saw those Vegas women hanging over the top of the dugout.

Paul Voigt asked, "Who are those chicks?"

I told him, "Just some schoolteachers!"

Back to the Albuquerque Dukes and the summer of 1983 in what ultimately would be my final game in the lineup with the Triple A Dodgers. The Dukes were playing Tacoma, and my roommate and lifetime friend, Paul Voigt, was the starting pitcher. Paul and I had a lot more in common other than playing with the Twins and our college degrees. Paul and John Franco were my roommates now in Albuquerque, and it was always an eventful time rooming with two New York boys, whose outlook on life differed from that of this lower Alabama boy. Paul really wanted a complete game this night and for sure the win. He was quite the competitor, and "Pauly," as he was affectionately nicknamed by Franco, always requested that I catch for him. There were many times when I would be in my catching position and I would put down every sign for every pitch Paul could possibly throw, only to have him shake off every pitch signal.

It was after the final shake-off on the last suggested pitch when Pauly gave this catcher a certain look that I was all too familiar with. I knew the next pitch from Pauly was going to knock the bat-ter down in the dirt or hit him right upside the helmet. I must have tackled half a dozen guys over the years who charged the mound on Paul Voigt after the Virginia graduate threw at them. He was quite the competitor on the mound, and he was not going to allow any hitter to get the best of him without throwing at least one pitch at the hitter's chin. Several times in games Pauly threw so far behind the hitter that it was completely obvious what he was doing. Paul didn't hit that many guys because I don't think he liked to fight. That was why he wanted me to catch his games since I was pretty good about tackling the batter before he reached the dirt of the mound in an effort to keep him off Paul.

That night, I was doing everything I could to keep Pauly in the game and get a complete game for him. But with one out and the score 2–1 in the bottom of the ninth, Paul had just walked Ricky Peters, the fastest guy on the Tacoma A's squad and the Pa-cific Coast League leader in stolen bases in 1983. I knew Paul was coming out of the game. I looked in the bullpen and saw Orel Her-shiser warming up, and then Del Crandall motioned for me to go and talk with Voigt.

That meant Del wanted me to steal some time with Paul in order to get Orel a few extra pitches in the bullpen. I knew that Orel had a much quicker delivery to the plate than Paul's methodical delivery. Al-ready that night, I had thrown Peters out once trying to steal, yet Ricky Peters had one stolen base off me or actually off Paul's slow delivery.

Now was my chance to do exactly what Del had preached to the team since spring training: either you fail or you succeed, but you will get the chance to compete. With Orel pitching, I had a great chance to throw the speedy Ricky Peters out this time. Destiny and Del Crandall were putting me into a situation to prove I could do it. This would give everyone important to my career a chance to see that my arm was back and I really was a good defensive catcher.

Hurrying to the mound, I heard Pauly already bitching, "This

SOB better not take me out of this game. This is my game to lose. I deserve a chance at a complete game."

I strongly said to him, "Paul, shut up and be quiet. You have pitched an awesome game, and Del wants Orel to get to the big leagues. You don't say a freakin' word when he comes out here. Don't you show up Del. Just give him the ball. You understand?"

Paul nodded, and we waited for Del as he laggardly walked to the mound.

Del walked up on the pitching rubber and said, "Paul, good job. I'm bringing Orel in to protect your win. Scotti, I'm bringing Jack in to catch!"

I couldn't believe it. I said, "What! You're bringing Jack in to catch right now in the middle of the ninth inning?"

Del stated, "Jack is throwing the ball real well. Do you have a problem with this?"

I said nothing more, and dispirited, I walked off the mound. I had never been taken out of a game in a situation like that nor had I ever seen a manager take a player out of a game for defensive purposes in that capacity, especially the catcher. There was no double switch, just complete removal. You don't even do that in Little League baseball!

I never meant to embarrass Del that night, but I was absolutely crushed, disheartened to the core, even to the point that I think I went into shock. On the way off the mound to the third base dugout, I took off all my catching gear and left a trail from the mound to the third base line, including my mitt and catcher's mask. If I had ample time before I reached the dugout, I think I would have stripped down to my underwear. Yet I did not ever remember leaving my catching gear on the field. The guys on the team had to tell me what I actually had done: I left a trail of clothes and catching gear, like Hansel and Gretel left bread crumbs, signifying my walk from the pitching rubber to third base steps. I didn't even remember walking off the field.

I felt like my own father told me to my face, "I do not believe in you anymore!" I walked right to my locker and didn't move.

Other players came to console me: "I can't believe Del did that." "That was bullshit what he did." But I remembered little after the initial shock of being pulled from the game.

Orel ended up throwing one pitch, and the batter grounded into a double play. Paul Voigt got his victory; Ricky Peters never ran to second base; and Jack Fimple never got a chance to throw the runner out!

Dukes pitching coach Brent Strom came to get me after the game; Del wanted to see me.

I fired back at Brent, "If Del can come and get me off the mound, then he can come to my locker and get me."

Well, Del did, and we went into the manager's office, anticipating nothing more than a sad ending. Del tried to reason his decision with this Dukes catcher, but it got no further than my shaking my head in disbelief. Our future together as aspiring coach and dedicated player was over.

I told Del that I believed his every word and would play in a forest fire for him. But now I wanted to go back to Double A to get more playing time. I was willing to step back a level to get more time behind the plate, something I was lacking on this stacked Albuquerque Dukes team. Truth be told, I no longer believed in Del, and I couldn't play for a manager I didn't believe in.

Even after this Greek tragedy played out, one week later I was still with the team. It was a long, grueling week, no at bats and nothing but bullpen work, and I resorted to soul-searching thoughts and prayer the entire road trip. I had Granny, whom I loved so dearly, praying for me. The question at hand was, Should I quit if the Dodgers didn't send me back to Double A?

The last game on the road was in Tucson, Arizona, and after the last inning, I packed my Dukes uniform, placing it in my private luggage to take it back to the apartment. I would personally give it to Pat McKernan, Albuquerque's general manager, the next day.

On the getaway morning, I said my good-byes to roommates Paul Voigt and the great left-handed reliever, John Franco, and headed to the Dukes front offices. Only Pauly and Johnny knew I was quitting and starting the trek of shame to my parents' home in Lillian, Alabama.

Walking into Pat's office, I was as downtrodden as anyone who ever entered through the general manager's door. The Albuquerque Dukes uniform was in a brown paper bag, and I laid it on Pat's desk.

McKernan was one of the pioneers of Minor League baseball. He won the John P. McPhail Trophy twice for best Minor League executive, making him the only two-time winner. He also won *The Sporting News* Minor League executive of the year on two occasions.

But he was a much greater man than just a good general manager of a Minor League club. Pat had a heart for people, and that day Pat had a heart for me.

I told Pat my point of view on the Del Crandall incident, which Pat was well aware of since he witnessed Del take me out of the game.

Pat just listened, and then he did what Pat did best: he offered hope! He spent the next thirty minutes trying to convince me to give it a little more time. Don't give up just yet!

We shook hands and said good-bye, and as I was walking out the door, the general manager's phone rang. On the other end was Bill Schweppe, head of the Minor Leagues for the Dodgers. I could hear Pat telling Mr. Schweppe that, yes, he would get in touch with Scotti Madison, and yes, he would tell Scotti to pack his bags and meet the San Antonio Dodgers on the road in El Paso, Texas. Can you believe that? A miracle phone call occurred at just the right time!

If I had walked out the door thirty seconds sooner, I never would have played in the Major Leagues. Yet of even greater significance, if Pat McKernan hadn't cared enough about me to talk with me that day, I would have left thirty minutes earlier. Bill Schweppe's call to this Dukes catcher would have gone unanswered.

We did not have cell phones back in 1983, and if the Dodgers had tracked me down at my parents' home, Bill Schweppe would have told me to just stay home. I am convinced to this day that God worked through the heart of the Albuquerque Dukes general manager, Pat McKernan, just like he worked through the heart of Baseball Chapel's Bob Smith in Clearwater, Florida. Two men, years apart, both sensitive to the whisper of God!

Looking back, I recognized that so often we easily give up on our dreams, but if we can just hold on a little longer, we will get the call we have been waiting on at just the right moment. I was just a phone call away from working in the Lunch Box League, but instead I would still be chasing my boyhood dreams, thanks to a big man with an even bigger heart, Pat McKernan.

I took off that late afternoon in the summer of 1983 for the 266-mile trip to meet my new team on the road in El Paso. The moon never looked so radiant emerging through the clouds that evening, and my future once again never looked so bright. As the air rushed carelessly through the open window, the thought of Kent Hrbek's being called to the Major Leagues in 1981 crossed my mind, and I was encouraged once more to carry onward. I still was just a phone call away from living my dreams.

Chapter 12

Walk of Shame

At Twins spring training every year, like every professional ball team in America, players are sent home because they did not make the cut. Some guys truly reached their potential years earlier, and others perhaps really didn't get a fair shake at camp. Whatever the case, leaving the ball fields, possibly for the last time in a career, is the most heart-wrenching day in any player's life.

Seldom have I seen a player walk away angry. I saw total desolation of the spirit. The first noticeable melancholy feeling was that of rejection, then a feeling of inadequacy, and in short order, deep, brokenhearted depression. The player ultimately reached a point in time when the door to his childhood dream was completely shut; a dream he'd had as long as he could remember, back to the day when he first held a ball, was over.

In the Twins Minor League locker room, within three weeks of opening practice, the cuts began. For veteran spring players who had previously witnessed players "walk the plank" in camps, the trepidation of hearing your name called out over a loudspeaker during breakfast brought your heartbeat to a halt.

My first recollection of being a part of the cut occurred while sitting at the breakfast table in Melbourne, the spring of 1981. We were all having lighthearted conversations, joking about the poor quality of food, when the intercom system was first turned on in the dining room. It was a scratchy sound, shaking off the rust of an off-season, immediately followed by a high-pitched sound that is consistent with cheap electronic equipment. If you have ever watched movies involving prisoners of war, you can get a feel about the atmosphere that spring day in Melbourne, when "the voice" broadcasting completely silences every other sound within earshot.

The movies depict prisoners strolling throughout the prison yard when the loudspeaker begins to announce the dreadful news of the day. A cloud of pessimism settles in on the survivors, while those struck with shock upon hearing their names start the humbling experience of walking to meet their Maker. In spring training, to a ballplayer it was worse than facing death; you were going home; you were released!

Such would be the case that day in Melbourne when your roommate, your teammate, and often your friend heard their names broadcast and got up and walked out of the room, and you never saw them again. The voice, like the man's voice behind the curtain in the *Wizard of Oz,* hovered above the room: "Attention, attention, would the following players please report to the Twins front offices," and then the list was slowly read.

As the names were called out, your eyes found the center of your plate, and you never looked up. You dared not look up as you heard chairs sliding out from the table, when released players stood up and carried their trays to the trash. They sadly began the walk of shame out of the dining room and headed directly to Mr. Rantz's office. Just like in the movie *The Green Mile,* "Dead man walking, dead man walking," was what every player in the room felt that moment.

If you were lucky, you might not have to go through the embarrassment of public humiliation, and "the voice" might have mistakenly overlooked your name at breakfast, or they decided to release you after breakfast began. It was only a brief reprieve, however; the Grim Reaper was waiting for you in the locker room. If you were not released at breakfast due to an oversight, then Wayne "Big Fella" Hattaway stopped by your locker and told you, "Mr. Rantz wants to see you," as he handed you a green trash bag so you could pack your personal gear. The bags were of poor quality, but at that moment in time, you didn't have the heart to ask for two so you could double up and take home your misery.

The fear that overcame every player as Big Fella walked around the locker room was gut wrenching. He had dozens of plastic trash bags hanging out of his front pocket and traversed from aisle to aisle, laying out trash bags for the ill-fated. When you knew a teammate had been notified of his release, you might walk up to him and calmly shake his hand and say, "I am sorry." Yet nothing you could say would bring comfort to the discouraged soul.

Often the fortunate ones still left would quickly get dressed and leave his presence, hoping that might ease some of his pain. Others dressed farther away as if the person being released had leprosy. It was mind-boggling to have a roommate who shared a room with you for three to four weeks; ate every meal with you; woke up and went to sleep with you at the same time; walked to the yard with you; and then his name was called over the intercom system, and you never saw him again.

I detested that part of spring training, and it brought on tremendous anxiety and eventually fever blisters on my lips. I experienced fever blisters on my lips for the next ten years in a row, all occurring the last week in the month of March.

After I played for Terry Collins and the San Antonio Dodgers the summer of '83, I was sold to another team in spring training. I was sitting in the Dodgers' cafeteria eating one of those fine Dodgers' omelets, and I was pondering my lot with the organization. I knew I didn't fit the mold of a Dodger, and I knew I would either be stuck in Double A the upcoming season or be released on one of the last days of camp. My run-in with Del Crandall had occurred the season before, so now I had no one in the Dodger organization who believed in me. I was just praying that an opportunity to play for another organization would come along before I entered the Lunch Box League.

While I was sitting there at breakfast with my roomie Paul Voigt, Bill Schweppe, head of the Minor Leagues, came up to our table with some news: "Scotti, I've got some good news for you. We just sold your contract to the Detroit Tigers. We thank you for playing hard for our organization. Good luck!"

I looked at Pauly in disbelief and then turned to Mr. Schweppe. I said, "Wait a minute, Mr. Schweppe. I am no longer a Dodger, and I am now with the Tigers?"

"That is what I said, son. Good luck." Then Mr. Schweppe began to walk away.

Quickly, I caught up with him in the hallway and asked, "Hey, Mr. Schweppe, how much did you get for me? How much was I worth?"

Bill Schweppe told me that he was not at liberty to reveal that information.

I was quite tenacious and was not going to let go of Mr. Schweppe's throat until I found out how much the Dodgers received for my contract.

Finally, Mr. Schweppe had enough of me and reluctantly relinquished the confidential information to this new Tigers catcher, "We got $10,000, and we think we got a good deal!"

As Bill Schweppe walked out the door for the very last time I would see him, this twenty-five-year-old responded to the eye-opening information: "That's it? That's all you got for me? $10,000. Are you kidding me? Surely there was another player involved!"

After I packed my bags that morning, I drove to Lakeland, Florida, the home of the Detroit Tigers. I would be walking into Tiger Town with a humble spirit. I was the only person I knew who had been bought for the price of $10,000!

☎

Fortunately, I was never released from a team and sent home from spring camp, unlike so many others. But many times I witnessed the feeling of total despair in the eyes of friends. Being released from any sports team toughens a man and prepares him for other disappointments in life, which are sure to come. I felt equally bad in the upcoming years when I personally experienced demotions, as well as being completely released from a team at the end of the season. The pain a player feels in a release is likened to the loss of a loved one in the death of a family member. Yet it feels worse than death, for in death hopefully the chosen one goes to heaven. In baseball, the released player has to face his family and friends and explain why he didn't make it. It is hard to admit, "I wasn't good enough."

☎

It was Friday, March 30, 1984, three years away from Twins spring camp, when I witnessed the most unforgettable demotion I ever saw in a spring camp. I was playing in the Minor Leagues with Detroit, and the Tigers spring camp ball fields were located about two hundred yards just beyond the right outfield wall of the Detroit Tigers spring stadium, Merchant Field.

As Minor League players, we found it both disheartening and highly motivating in one swoop to be practicing on the Minor League fields and hear the cheers right next door coming from the big league stadium. You could hear the public address system over the practice fields announcing, "Now batting, Kirk Gibson, Kirk Gibson," and it would send chills up your spine. Thus, as a Minor League player, you were arm's length away every day from your dreams. You seemed so close to stardom practicing next to the big league team, yet you were so far away at times, daily facing the reality of Minor League baseball.

Speaking of dreams, I decided to go and say good-bye to Jim "Dream" Weaver on this particular last day of big league camp. The Tiger squad of 1984 was breaking north, and the bus was pulling out at 8:00 a.m., taking the team to the charter flight to play one more exhibition game in Cincinnati before arriving in Detroit later in the evening. The players were in their coats and ties, the customary dress that Sparky Anderson required when a Tigers player traveled anywhere, even out of the hotel room.

Opening day was to begin on April 3, and the team was etched in stone. My friend Dream Weaver played with me in Orlando, as well as in Visalia, and Weaver was traveling north with the big league team.

Jim had been purchased from the Cleveland Indians' roster, and he was in a great position. If he did not make the Tigers camp from spring camp, he would be sold back to the Indians' twenty-five-man roster for half the purchase price or something like that, according to Jim. The roster had been set by end of the business day, one day earlier, so everyone knew who was on the team.

The night before camp broke, I joined Weaver and patronized Hooters. Almost the entire big league team was in attendance, celebrating the end of spring training. The Hooters in Lakeland was one of the first in the franchise, if not the very first. Prior to Hooters, it was unheard of to patronize a bar that had sports on TV and served wings and beer, delivered by scantily clothed girls. So, it was the most popular place in Lakeland for Tigers ballplayers and other men in general.

That night, the Tigers team ate all the oysters and chicken wings in the place and finished them off with a handsome amount of cold ones. They had earned their stripes in camp, and by the time the upcoming 1984 season would end, they would become World Champions. I was a participant in the festivities, and the guys bought me a fair share of adult beverages to enjoy.

Thus, witnessing their morning departure, I was quite familiar with why everyone was so quiet walking onto the bus. Every one of the previous night's participants was covering red eyes from the light of day, even though it was completely overcast. If someone had accidentally scratched the eyes of either of my two favorite players, Alan Trammell and Darrell Evans, that morning, he would have bled to death.

I drove over from Minor League camp next door to see the team off. As I was saying good-bye to Jim Weaver that day, I noticed Mike Laga and Doug Baker placing their luggage in the compartment under the bus. Doug was as good a defensive shortstop as you could be, and first baseman Mike Laga hit massive home runs. In fact, on September 15, 1986, Laga would become the only player to ever hit the ball completely out of the Cardinals' Busch Stadium. The fans gave him a standing ovation. So what if it was a foul ball? It left the entire yard, a remarkable feat. In other words they were good players, and along with Jim and all the Hooter's flu-ridden players, they made the Tigers big league squad, at least until 7:55 a.m. It was then that they were escorted off the bus!

I had just gotten into my car and was leaving the Tigers' parking lot to head back to Fetzer Hall, the building where the Minor League players ate breakfast every morning. Jim Schmakel, the greatest equipment manager ever in the game of baseball, had just walked onto the bus, and Doug Baker and Mike Laga were following Jim off the bus.

Sensing something was up, I decided to stay in the parking lot and watch the course of events evolving right before me. That morning I missed breakfast, but I would never forget the moment when I watched Baker and Laga crawl underneath the bus to retrieve their luggage, which they had packed fifteen minutes earlier. The forever lasting impression on my memory was seeing both men, luggage in hand, eating the exhaust fumes from the Tigers' team bus as it left the parking lot headed to the Orlando International Airport.

There had been a trade that morning, which brought the Tigers a couple of new players, simultaneously sealing the fate of Baker and Laga. They had become expendable, and the next bus ride they would take would ferry them to Toledo, Ohio, a league away from the Major Leagues. I watched what appeared to be two dejected players standing beside their bags, staring in the direction of the departing buses, probably wondering, *This has got to be a bad dream!*

Both players finally regained their senses, slowly awakening from their nightmare, after what seemed to be an eternity of silence. Shoulders slumped over and with no sense of urgency, they dragged their bags across the parking lot; Laga was dragging his on its side. They took the two-hundred-yard walk across the parking lot to the Minor League facility, first stopping at Fetzer Hall, where all the other Minor League players were eating breakfast. What a walk of shame!

With a melancholy feeling smothering their emotions, Baker and Laga joined their new brothers that day. They were the only players during the entire spring camp who ate breakfast at Fetzer Hall while wearing coats and ties!

Chapter 13

There Are No Rules

B ack to Twins camp. Spring training of 1981 was almost over, and the teams were set; each player was now practicing with the final team in which he would soon break camp. The alignment had occurred, and the powers that be had players exactly where they wanted them to start the 1981 season.

Herbie and I were with the Single A team, the Visalia Oaks, and we spoke with our manager, Dick Phillips, for the very first time. Although "Skip," as he liked to be called, had been coaching in spring camp, neither of us had any prior dealings with him since we had been practicing daily with the Mud Hens manager, Cal Ermer, and a totally different set of players. Now demoted and demoralized, we were being shipped out to Visalia, California.

If there was ever a manager just perfect in managerial style and laid-back demeanor for a specific team, Dick Phillips was the ideal skipper for the Visalia Oaks. Richard Eugene Phillips was a native of Racine, Wisconsin, and was fifty years of age at the time he managed the Oaks ball club. He stood about six feet tall and might have weighed all of 180 pounds after half a dozen beers. Skip's carefree management style was just what this bunch of independent, rebellious, and hard-driving ballplayers needed.

I would play for competitive Minor League teams, but none would have as much drive to win a championship as this one would. Most of the new 1981 Visalia Oaks players felt like they got screwed and should have started at a higher classification to begin the season, so they all showed up with a chip on their shoulders. Herbie and I had hit extremely well in camp, yet now we felt like filling up the air with upper cuts when we met our new teammates due to our demotion!

In the first team meeting, Dick Phillips welcomed the team and started by announcing he wanted to go over his team rules. This announcement immediately didn't sit well with either Herbie or me, much less with any other newly appointed Visalia Oaks player that morning in Melbourne, Florida. *Rules! Rules! We don't need no stinking rules!* Then Phillips hit a home run with his team when he stated, "Most of you guys are probably pissed off that you are here in Single A ball and feel like you deserve better. I'm pissed off too! I should be managing in the Major Leagues. This game is tough, so I understand if you are all pissed off. Yet I still have to go over my rules. I don't really have any rules. We are just going to play hard and have fun!" Skip never smiled as he brought us this welcomed message. He delivered it in the tone of a matter-of-fact message, and we could sense the honesty in his speech.

Standing on the pitching mound at the Twins spring training camp, Dick Phillips was an instant hit with his team, and any resentment a guy felt about starting in Single A Visalia, California, was tossed right out the window. Our baseball spirits were awakened, and we felt energized to play baseball once again. We would break as a team and continue that closeness throughout the upcoming 1981 season. We would play hard, we would have fun, and we would win!

The number one individual goal of every Minor League player is to get the call to make it to the Major Leagues. Thus, due to self-seeking ambitions, baseball quickly becomes a more individual sport rather than the team sport every fan so desperately desires. That would not be the case for the Visalia Oaks players. Each of us wanted a day in the big leagues, but each one of us wanted to win and we just liked playing baseball. I never heard a player during the entire season discuss advancing to the next level or saw a locker buddy act envious over a teammate's individual success.

We congruently possessed a mean spirit on the field against all our competition. The Oaks players just wanted to win, and Phillips was smart enough to get out of our way, provide occasional advice, and treat us like a bunch of big leaguers. Skip didn't care what we did either before or after every game. He only wanted results, and his players, through great team effort and career seasons for some, would soon give Dick Phillips a dream season, winning 63 percent of our games in 1981.

☎

It was now time to break camp to begin this 1981 season, and Herbie and I were about to travel from Melbourne, Florida, to Visalia, California, a due west course. As Horace Greeley and John B. Soule so eloquently stated, "Go west, young man. If you have no family or friends to aid you . . . turn your face to the Great West and build up your home and fortune." Kent Hrbek was about to start the season of 1981, which would build up his home and begin his fame and fortune.

After the last morning spring practice, Herbie and I took off to Visalia, California, riding in his late 1970s Ford F-150 truck, complete with white camper shell. We were part of a caravan of four vehicles that consisted of Paul Voigt, Joe Kubit, and Kenny "Chief" Francingues. According to Rand McNally, the trip was about 2,674 miles if you take the shortest route, taking you on I-20 through Dallas and on to Albuquerque on I-40. Of course, that would have been the best route if we had known someone in Dallas and Albuquerque where we could crash.

There were two problems with our navigation strategies. First, we did not have Internet or Garmins, so we relied on the free paper maps we took from either AAA or gas stations. Second, we road warriors had friends only in New Orleans, Louisiana, Houston, Texas, and Phoenix, Arizona, so those were places we could count on to eat a hot meal, crash, and sleep on our friends' couches and floors. Remember we had almost no money, and the Twins gave each car driver about $250 in travel money to make ends meet.

I told the Twins I was riding with Herbie, so management gave me additional cash. Those extra dollars served us quite well. This

Road warriors: left to right: Paul Voigt, Joe Kubit, Joe's wife,
Kenny "Chief" Francingues, and Kent Hrbek.

was an era that emphasized personal responsibility, and an individual needed to know when to say no. This was also a time in history when drinking while driving was kosher. So when you combined the two and then applied those principles to two twenty-one-year-olds who liked to play hard, both on and off the field, you ended up with two ballplayers who consumed three cases of beer en route to their destination.

Due to excessive fun, Herbie's and my trip ended up maybe two days longer than it should have been. There was the detour just outside Phoenix, which took us to Las Vegas, that added to the tardy arrival. Oh, yeah, then there was extra time spent when we stopped everywhere along the way we saw people swimming in a river or a creek to take a dip.

The first overnight stop for the caravan of players was at my home in Lillian, Alabama. My mom and dad were out of town; I so wished that my dad could have met some of my new teammates. Paul Voigt, a graduate of Virginia, would soon become one of my best friends, and Pauly later became one of my dad's favorites. Pauly would spend two weeks with me in the spring of 1982 before we would attend the Dodgers big league camp. Being a Long Island resident brought with it snow and cold weather during the months prior to spring training, so Pauly's trip down south to the panhandle of Florida served both of us well.

My father seldom missed one of my games; he traveled everywhere to watch me play. Dad was a great ballplayer in high school and college. He played football, baseball, and basketball at Atmore, Alabama, High, and then he attended the University of Georgia on a football scholarship. Imagine all those games he played throughout the years, and imagine your parents never attending one game. That was what my father wrestled with all his life. He was determined he would not miss seeing me play as a way to make up for something his parents never gave him. Due to economic reasons, however, my parents were unable to travel to California for the upcoming season, and it would be the first and only time my dad would miss an entire season of watching me play.

Mom, Sandra Madison, was also a huge fan of mine; she came into my life at a later age. I lost a mom and a sister in a car accident when I was ten years old, which probably led to some of my success as a driven player. It is only natural to gravitate to a sport and bury your inward pains in the effort and dedication it takes to be successful. Sandra Madison was also an angel whom God brought me when I was twelve years old, and she came in the form of a stepmom, a name I never used to refer to her. She was Mom early on and brought stability to our family, and she directed us to the front doors of church on a regular basis. She also kept my dad calm at times when he might otherwise have blown his top. They both would have enjoyed my friends and would have fixed us one huge

southern breakfast as a parting gift for the upcoming season. Fortunately, my sister, Ann, replaced their hospitality with some of
her own, and we departed for the West with full stomachs to grab
unfulfilled dreams.

After a South Alabama breakfast, the caravan had lunch in New
Orleans with Kenny Francingues's family. Kenny, known by his
teammates as Chief, was through and through a full-blooded Ca-
jun, and his family put on a meal for the group that was straight
from Paul Prudhomme's favorite recipes, sprinkled with some
Italian dishes around the table. We were so full that I thought we
would have to take a nap before we took off for Houston, Texas.
Houston was our next stop, where we stayed at the condo of my
high school sweetheart.

We were road warriors, and I felt we were much like Grateful
Dead groupies traveling and stopping in on friends and acquain-
tances, needing a place to shower and crash before the next adventure rolled us onward chasing The Dead.

Kent Hrbek in the great state of Texas.

Chapter 14

Baseball, Apple Pie, and Country Music

erbie's Ford truck traveled through lots of small towns across Louisiana, Texas, and New Mexico, and it seemed as if we were changing the radio station for better reception about every thirty minutes. Most radio channels in that part of the country proudly carried country tunes. Before college, I was a total rock-and-roll listener, but then I became a fan of country music, especially due to the friends I met while living in Nashville, Tennessee.

I had lots of time to talk with my new buddy, and after hearing a Charlie Daniels's tune on the radio, I proceeded to tell Kent about the music entertainers I befriended at Vanderbilt and the unlikely stories that went along with them. What I thought was especially neat about these entertainers is that they all loved baseball. It started first with Jerry Reed, my favorite!

Jerry Reed was a real trip, and he loved to laugh. What you saw of him in the movie *Smokey and the Bandit* was what I saw regularly at Jerry's home. I first met Jerry when I was being recruited by Vanderbilt to play football.

Back in 1976, it was perfectly legal for university-appointed people to call a recruit on the phone and try to convince him to come to their college, in this case Vanderbilt. The recruiting coordinator then for Vanderbilt was also the baseball coach, Larry Schmittou. Coach Schmittou later went on to establish the Nashville Sounds, selecting financial partners in the country music industry, all of whom he first met through Vanderbilt.

The athletic marketers came up with this idea to get country music stars to help out the Vanderbilt football program. Since most entertainers were not any different from most professional baseball players, they did not have college degrees, thus no particular universities to rally around. Jerry Reed was one star who agreed to help Vanderbilt, and he called me on a regular basis during my senior year in high school. Coach Schmittou wanted me badly since I also played baseball. Thus, it would save Schmittou a baseball scholarship if I would sign on a football scholarship and also play baseball for Schmittou.

Well, I eventually enrolled at Vanderbilt, thanks to Jerry's calls, and then the fun really started. I stopped by Jerry's house pretty much at will, and Prissy, Jerry's devoted wife, often fixed something for me to eat. Prissy was not only a sweet lady; she was quite talented musicwise as well. She had been a backup singer for Elvis Presley in younger days, and that was how she and Jerry met. Many times other folks were visiting Jerry, such as actor Burt Reynolds or singer-songwriter Ray Stevens. Jerry's sidekick role with Burt, as Cledus "Snowman" Snow, catapulted his popularity in the entertainment world overnight. He was already a great country artist, but he became a movie star too. And this notoriety occurred when I was taking my journey through Vanderbilt.

One trip I took with Jerry and his lovely daughter Sedina was to the Oklahoma State Fair. We traveled in a Learjet, which was this Vanderbilt freshman's first experience living like a rock star.

On the way back from Oklahoma City, I noticed a phone in the jet. I asked Jerry, "Does this phone work?"

"Sure, who do you want to call?" he said.

I told Jerry that I hadn't called Granny in quite some time, and I promised her I would call her over the weekend.

Jerry said, "Let's give Granny a call!"

When I got Granny on the phone, I explained that I was calling from a jet: "Granny, hey, I'm in a Learjet thirty thousand feet in the air. And I'm riding with Jerry Reed!"

Granny found it hard to believe, even though I kept repeating, "I'm in a Learjet with Jerry Reed!"

Finally, Jerry said, "Give me that phone. Granny, this is Jerry Reed! When you're hot, you're hot!"

Granny was then completely convinced that her grandyoung-un was with Jerry Reed, and for the next ten minutes she asked all about Jerry's family and where he grew up. Jerry spoke with her just like she was his own granny. Granny told him she loved his new movie, *Smokey and the Bandit*.

When Jerry later moved to Franklin, Tennessee, I found some animal mounts for him in Alaska. I was traveling in Alaska playing baseball from Kenai to Fairbanks, and I called Jerry when I saw a beautiful trophy mount, in particular a white timber wolf hide. Jerry sent money through Western Union, and I shipped the immaculate hide to Jerry's front door all the way from Palmer, Alaska. Jerry liked baseball and he liked me, so I kept him abreast of my progress throughout the years.

☎

As we made our way down the road through Texas, I kept talking to Herbie, but he made no comment whatsoever, other than shake his head, probably in disbelief. The road trip story then moved from guitar-playing Jerry Reed to the greatest fiddle player of that day, Charlie Daniels. We were heading due west on Interstate I-10, and Herbie finally looked away from the road after this name caught his attention.

The story began when I was Charlie Daniels's catcher in a celebrity softball game. I was in my dorm room at Vanderbilt when I received a call from a man introducing himself as Charlie Daniels's road manager. He informed me that they needed some ringers to beef up Charlie's team: Was I available to play in a celebrity softball game next Saturday in Chattanooga, Tennessee?

I couldn't believe what I was hearing. Getting to play on the same team with Charlie Daniels? Could this guy be for real?

For the past four Octobers, I sat in my car outside a Nashville auditorium and turned the radio dial to listen to the Volunteer Jam. The Volunteer Jam was the annual Charlie Daniels Band concert first held on October 4, 1974, at the War Memorial Auditorium in Nashville, Tennessee. It was the beginning of a great tradition in music thanks to Charlie. I couldn't afford to buy a ticket, so the next best thing was to park my car in a lot adjacent to the auditorium. I managed to find a strategic spot underneath some magnolia trees in the parking lot of a retirement home. From this vantage point, I could almost recognize the songs being played in the auditorium. I flipped back and forth from my radio playing the live event to the live sound of cheering fans happening some seventy-five yards away in the auditorium.

The greatest benefit from my parked location was watching the limousines roll up to the back door, dropping off the performers. Over the four-year period I "attended" the concert, I swore I saw Jimmy Hall, Dickey Betts, Dobie Gray, the Allman Brothers Band, the Marshall Tucker Band, Billy Joel, Stevie Ray Vaughan, Ted Nugent, Alabama, Don Henley, and Barefoot Jerry climb out of their limos, and a few minutes later, they were bigger than life playing their songs on my radio! I thought that was so cool, and I dreamed I would one day meet some of those famous entertainers. Thus, I thought quite highly of the great Charlie Daniels, and now I was about to be his battery mate in a celebrity softball game.

The manager told me to wait outside my dorm room, and the bus would pick me up at nine o'clock on Saturday morning. I packed all my baseball gear that morning and stood outside Vanderbilt's Carmichael Towers on West End Avenue. I was really hoping this was not a cruel joke from a friend, who may have disguised his voice two days earlier. I kept looking in both directions, and there in the distance, I saw a motor coach approaching. It came to a stop in front of my catching bag.

A man stuck his head out the bus door and said, "Jump on board."

It wasn't Jerry Reed's Learjet, but it was my first motor coach ride, and I enthusiastically climbed aboard.

The first person I met was Charlie Daniels himself, comfortably seated in a lounge chair. I had no idea I would ride with Charlie and sit with him in the front of the bus for the next two hours. Charlie and I talked about baseball all the way to Chattanooga. Even with all his success and fame, he possessed a humble spirit and treated me like I was somebody.

To this day I don't know whether we won or lost, but I took away two favorite memories from the day. The first was walking out to the mound and telling Charlie, "You don't have to apologize to the hitters every time you don't give them a good pitch to hit." The next was when Charlie asked if I had a favorite song he could play for me in the concert following the game. I requested "Long Haired Country Boy."

Charlie smiled, shook my hand, and on stage that day played "Long Haired Country Boy" after announcing to the crowd, "This song is dedicated to our catcher on my softball team, All-SEC player Scotti Madison!" I never saw or spoke to Charlie Daniels again. I didn't need to, for my love for baseball had given me another lasting memory!

☎

Somewhere in the story about Charlie Daniels, a song came on the radio sung by the Oak Ridge Boys. I told Kent I would get back to them in a minute, after Charlie's story was over. At the time, the Oak Ridge Boys' new hit "Elvira" was launched in the baseball season of 1981 and was a number one country song and crossed over to number five on the pop charts.

I first met the Oak Ridge Boys in the dugout of a Vanderbilt baseball game a year earlier. Two of the Oaks, Joe Bonsall and Richard Sterban, were huge baseball fans, and they often wore Philly jerseys on stage. Duane Allen and William Lee Golden, the self-proclaimed mountain man, also talked baseball with me and fully appreciated those who had the talent to play the game and play it well. I was invited out on the tour bus with the Oaks for several years, making some half dozen trips. I enjoyed them and found them to be great guys, "guys' guys," and always most accommodating to me and my friends.

I liked all the guys, but William Lee spoke to me most often about the deeper subject matters during my friendship with the Oaks. I eventually went by William Lee's historic home in Hendersonville and gave him rides to catch the tour bus. However, our first encounter was quite interesting, to say the least, and I was most uncomfortable with the stare that William Lee gave me.

We were sitting in the very back of the Oaks bus, and Golden was stroking his famous beard from top to bottom. The entire time he stared at me, never cracked an expression or said a word, and never batted an eye. I knew William Lee grew up in Brewton, Alabama, not far from my home in Pensacola, Florida. I also knew from a young age that you have to learn to relate to people. This philosophy was later reinforced by Professor Bobby Brooks at Vanderbilt, who said, "Class, I don't care who your mommy is or

Randy Owen of Alabama and William Lee Golden of the Oak Ridge Boys
on a trip I took with the Oaks.

who your daddy is or how much your trust fund is when you get out of Vanderbilt. If you can't learn to relate to people, you're not going to make it in this world!"

Professor Brooks's words rang true to me. Relating to people comes from the heart, and talking with them about something they enjoy is part of that. You don't start off talking to William Lee Golden about music no more than you discuss football with Coach Nick Saban. They don't want to talk about their jobs. Yes, these are exceptional people whose dedication to excellence has taken them to the top of their fields. But they are normal people who appreciate the simple pleasures in life like everybody else, probably even more so.

I asked William Lee, "Did you go to W. S. Neal or T. R. Miller?" referring to the local high schools in Brewton, Alabama.

William Lee replied, "T. R. Miller!"

Then I asked the all-important question you ask a big fellow born and raised in the state of Alabama, "Were you the left tackle or right tackle on offense or defense?"

William Lee Golden replied with a growing smile on his face: "I went both ways!"

Laughter erupted in the back of the bus, and our friendship was sealed. I cherished those days of traveling with such music stars and friends like the Oaks, who were down-to-earth folks and, most important to me, friends of mine and fans of baseball.

Herbie finally turned to me and expressed himself as he did when he was excited for me: "No shit, Chuck!"

About that time a Jerry Reed song hit the airways, and we saw the first signs for Houston, Texas. We were heading due west but started singing, "East bound and down, loaded up and truckin', we're gonna do what they say can't be done."

I relished the moment and had a feeling of contentment. I was certainly proud of my Vanderbilt diploma, but the experiences in my life, considered by many as out of the ordinary, left everlasting memories for me. Who would ever believe all that had happened to me? Certainly not my teammates! Would my children I might one day have believe all my crazy stories? Maybe Herbie would? Even if the big kid from Minnesota thought I was a little crazy, at least it was making for an interesting trip.

Chapter 15
Nothing Leaves Vegas

After Houston, the next overnight stay for Herbie and me was
Phoenix, Arizona, and an old college friend of Paul's supplied
the home for our encampment. She turned out to be the most
beautiful and sharpest girl we would meet for the entire summer
of 1981, and I always wondered why I never called her back to say
hello at the end of the baseball season.

Her name was Kathy Geraise, and she was the personification of
class. Pauly gave her his blue Twins baseball jersey that he had stolen three days earlier from Minor League camp. She wore it proudly, and Pauly might have even told her he was on his way to the

Left to right: Bill Geraise, Paul Voigt, and Kathy Geraise.
The Geraises were our hosts in Phoenix, Arizona.

big leagues. It was as good a line as any, and many a Minor League player probably threw out that same hook once or twice.

At this point, the caravan parted ways. The other guys headed straight to Visalia, by way of Los Angeles. Herbie and I took a detour to Las Vegas.

A sign outside Phoenix read:

KINGMAN 20

LAS VEGAS 115

LOS ANGELES 368

Seeing that was all we needed to convince us to take a detour to Las Vegas. After all, it was closer according to the sign; there are so many unknowns in life, and we might never get another chance to visit Vegas. And besides, if we were late showing up in Visalia, Dick Phillips already told us he didn't have any rules.

We were excited and turned the beer drinking up a notch. But before we entered the dazzling lights of Sin City, we ventured over to Hoover Dam. I talked Herbie into visiting Lake Mead and the dam, but neither of us had any idea of the beauty of those sites. We could not get over how awesome Hoover Dam was, and we sat on the edge of the dam and tossed coins over the side for some thirty minutes. That was long before the towel-headed fanatics blew up the Twin Towers in New York City, so back then, you could literally walk across the dam and stand on the edge. Along with the Sequoia National Forest outside Visalia, it was one of the favorite sites that I visited in the summer of 1981. We took photos of the memory and headed into Vegas on a high note.

We felt quite important when the dark blue Ford F-150 pulled up to valet parking at Caesars Palace. We were in awe looking at the Roman columns and statues peppering the grounds of Caesars Palace. It was hard to believe this hotel started from money, $35 million to be exact, loaned from the Teamsters' Central States

Herbie and Scotti at Hoover Dam.

Pension Fund. It had the look of organized crime all over it, which was probably why the Perlmans had to sell it in 1981.

The two boys sporting cutoff white baseball shorts got out of the Ford truck, tossed the keys to the valet, and checked into a room. After a well-deserved shower, we went out for a look-see of the strip and a few beers to keep us company. We didn't stay out long and were both dead asleep by midnight. The long trip from Melbourne was taking its toll on us, and the satisfaction of sleeping in a bed after two nights of restless sleep on the floor was a welcomed sensation.

We awoke the next morning after our bodies told us we had enough rest, and we headed out the doors on the final leg of the journey about 10:30 in the morning. We knew the breakfast buffet at Caesars would satisfy our hunger pains until we reached the

Los Angeles city limits. Soon we would be in Visalia, and the next stop was Recreation Park, our new baseball home for the next five months.

☎

Dick Phillips was anxiously waiting for us when we arrived one day late, yet in time to start the season. We caught a little heat from Phillips about arriving a day later than the rest of the team. When the caravan left Phoenix, we were nowhere to be found by our teammates, and since this was the age prior to cell phones, they didn't know how to get in touch with us. Paul Voigt and the gang assumed we would be in Visalia when the rest of the guys showed up.

When leaving Phoenix, we had no idea we were near Las Vegas until we saw the sign pointing the way to Sin City. It was a spur-of-the-moment decision, which probably worked out better as an excuse for us. We just told Phillips it was a long way from Melbourne to Visalia and we got lost. He didn't really care as long as we made opening day and, more important, hit just as well in Visalia as we batted earlier in spring training.

Chapter 16

Glory Days

Dick Phillips, a most likable man, was the ideal manager for the Visalia Oaks because of his laid-back personality and style. He even looked relaxed when he sat around the dugout; his face was elongated, his eyes were droopy looking, and he could have passed for the hound dog in the Hush Puppy shoe advertisements.

Phillips's playing career extended from 1951 through 1967, with time out for military service during the Korean War. An outfielder when he broke into baseball, he later was a first baseman and second baseman. I admired the man who spent his entire first decade in professional baseball in the Minor Leagues, mostly in the farm systems of the Milwaukee Braves and the San Francisco Giants. Phillips would win the 1961 Pacific Coast League Most Valuable Player award that gave the then thirty-year-old Phillips his first Major League opportunity, but he went hitless in three at bats and was returned to the Minors. The following season, the Giants sold Phillips's contract to the Washington Senators, and Phillips would spend the entire 1963 and 1964 campaigns on Washington's roster, starting sixty-seven games at first base for the 1963 Senators and fifty-two more there in 1964. He was a baseball lifer through and through!

Dick never told us about his time in the show. Oddly enough, I don't think I ever had a manager in the Minor Leagues who talked about his playing days in the big leagues. It was especially true of the younger coaches and managers when it came to sharing their personal playing time. It appeared to be such a taboo for managers or coaches to speak about their playing time. It was almost as if they were soldiers returning from a military campaign. It is a well-known occurrence that war veterans returning from military campaigns never discuss their combat missions or what transpired in heated skirmishes with the enemy. I assume it must be too painful to relive some of those terrible moments, and they wish they could have done something differently to change the outcome. I especially think rookie coaches who were forced to walk away from active play unfulfilled in their performance level wished they could have changed the outcome too.

Such was the lot of most Minor League managers. It became a mind game if you combined the regrets derived from lack of achievement with the cold, hard fact you are now a Minor League coach, and you get to pay your dues all over again for a slim chance of becoming a big league coach. Yet to seldom or never discuss your role as a Major League player with your players was just something I could not fully comprehend. Maybe it was because more times than not, the coach's career as a player was shortened or not quite as fulfilling as he had aspired it to be. His performance was too painful to discuss, and he felt like he never accomplished his goals as a player, thus his dreams were never satisfactorily fulfilled.

Realistically, not many Major League players play as long as they want to play, play on a championship team, or have the personal statistics that label them as exceptional. Most players who become coaches will walk away from the game unfulfilled, like 95 percent of the rest of the players; the majority leave frustrated and with more regrets than feelings of accomplishment. I guess even in life, everyone looks back and says, "I wish I could have done more!"

Early on in a rookie manager's career, it must be torture to manage a Minor League team filled with talented players, some who will probably accomplish more than you did in the show. It is a constant reminder that you were once just like them, yet your chance passed you by. Maybe there would be too many regrets, and it would be too painful to reminisce about glory days. Like Bruce Springsteen sang:

> *I had a friend was a big baseball player*
> *back in high school*

He could throw that speedball by you
Make you look like a fool boy
Saw him the other night at this roadside bar
I was walking in, he was walking out
We went back inside sat down had a few drinks
but all he kept talking about was:
Glory days well they'll pass you by
Glory days in the wink of a young girl's eye
Glory days, glory days

It would be a constant reminder every day you stepped on the field and thought, *What if?* I think it would be healthier for the soul to walk away from the game and try his hand at something else than to reminisce daily about glory days. Yet for most coaches, that was not an option. Staying in the game for some coaches, with the wealth of young talent on the field, was like serving time.

☎

Thus, Dick Phillips never spoke to us about his playing days, and none of us ever knew he had played once upon a time in the Major Leagues. Besides, after watching Skip toss batting practice, you would tend to believe that he never even played Little League baseball.

"Skip," as his players affectionately called him, may have been the worst batting practice pitcher of all time. His arm was shot, and every time he threw a pitch, my arm hurt just watching him. He stood fifteen feet in front of the mound hunched over and short armed the ball to home plate. The Visalia Oaks had one field manager, one bench coach, and one pitching coach, and it was Dick Phillips, all rolled up into a do-everything coach.

Skip was at a disadvantage when other teams in the California League had at least a second coach to assist the manager, which usually consisted of a pitching coach. Not the Twins! If you remember from spring camp, we did not have certified trainers in spring training, so there was no way they would pay for the services of an extra coach. If anything, a second coach provided someone with whom the manager could consult and seek additional advice about player decisions. Certainly four eyes were better than two when it came to evaluating performance.

Another reason for a second coach was that it eliminated the probability of the manager drinking alone, as Dick Phillips often would in Visalia. Skip could have used the company. With no other coaching arm to assist him, Skip was responsible for throwing batting practice (BP) every day of the season. Soon, however, he realized his arm was shot, and we needed another option for a batting practice pitcher. On the other hand, drinking alone for him was not a problem!

Thank God for Rick Kyzer, the Oaks utility infielder, and second baseman Tony Pilla. Rick tossed BP every day, and other players, mostly Pilla, chipped in. Then Skip could remain in the Oaks home team locker room with his door closed. He was known to sip a beer or two before and after games. He had a small Styrofoam cooler strategically placed at the far end of his desk, opposite the entrance to his offices. It held about six to eight beers daily along with a bag of ice. Even with his door closed, you could hear that pshhhhh sound a can of beer makes when it is opened. He was a good manager, and whatever he did never negatively affected his judgment on the field. We didn't care what Skip did before or after a game, just like he didn't care what we did. Just play ball!

Chapter 17

Roomies

The California League runs up and down the San Joaquin Valley and was often classified as a High Single A league, which means there was good talent playing on a daily basis. We played in towns like San Jose, Stockton, Modesto, Lodi, Fresno, Redwood City, and even Reno, our favorite. The reason Reno was the best town we played in was not due to gambling; it was the cheapest place we could eat. We were given $9 per day meal money, which does not go far, and Reno had lots of buffets and breakfast specials that were perfect for economically challenged baseball players.

The California League's history reached as far back as the late 1800s, and the current California League was formed in 1941. Visalia was now the Oaks, but previously had been called names such as the Rawhide, the Cubs, the Stars, the Redlegs, the A's, the White Sox, and the Mets before settling on the current name. Over time there had been thirty-two cities and towns that hosted a California League team, but the 1981 season involved only eight towns. It was a new part of the country that I had never seen, and I looked forward to the sights up and down California Highway 99.

Our team, like every sports team in America, was a melting pot for every type of kid, ranging from different races to varying socio-economic conditions in our upbringings. Most of us were probably making the minimum of $700 per month, and our highest-paid player might have been making $900 per month. Thank goodness we weren't charged for bats and balls, or there never would have been a Minor League team for the Twins.

Some of us had cars we had purchased with our signing bonuses, and we had them in Visalia. Yet most of the players needed to catch rides to the yard on a regular basis. The key to survival was finding good roommates, and I was fortunate in picking outfielder Jim Weaver and lefty pitcher Lee Belanger as my roomies for the summer of '81. We shared everything: utility bills, apartment rent, groceries, gas, and even a few dates with local Visalia girls, at least Jim and I did. One groupie Oaks fan often stopped by and cleaned our apartment. That was okay with us, and she appeared to be happy with feeling that she was able to help out some ballplayers. I later introduced her to Paul Voigt, and she cleaned his apartment occasionally.

It was nice to have fans! The three of us lived in a two-bedroom apartment to save on money, and the player who landed the single room was the one who either had a "special guest" coming out to

Left to right: roomies Jim "Dream" Weaver, Scotti, and Lee Belanger.

California for a visit or was the roomie who procured a special date after a weeknight game.

For the life of me I couldn't figure out how Jim's and Lee's bodies lasted the entire season. Every day when they woke up, they ate Captain Crunch cereal, dry. No milk! Go figure. And then around 2:00 p.m. they traveled to Mooney Boulevard and ordered a Moe's to Go sub sandwich, roast beef and pastrami. That was the diet every day for these two players when we were playing at home in Visalia.

☎

And then there was Charlie, Lee's parakeet, which stayed in the apartment. The bird was a constant chatterbox unless you covered his cage with a sheet. Charlie was also a veteran of spring camps and had made the trek from Lee's home in California to spring camp in Melbourne several times with Lee.

Once I got tired of the noise and hid Charlie in a neighbor's apartment. Lee came home to find out that I had gone to great lengths to prepare a Cornish hen with rice. I told Lee I had enough of Charlie and he might as well enjoy him one last time. The joke provided a good laugh for me, but only after Lee filled the room with upper cuts and expletives!

Chapter 18

Wolfy

There is no doubt, money was tight, but the puppy love that we still felt for the game helped us look beyond our dire financial difficulties. I think being in the Minor Leagues for some players was just a way to delay the inevitable, which was getting a real job, you know, the Lunch Box League, as pitching coach Jim Shellenback appropriately named it.

Soon into the 1981 season you could see the guys who were really struggling financially, mainly those who were already married and maybe had a child. One player, Larry May, the "Big Amish" as we called him, applied for food stamps to help support his wife and child, and the government granted his request. Guys took bread and jars of peanut butter on road trips to supplement their hunger pains and lack of funds.

The players who seemed to make it okay through the season without much financial headache were the guys who landed a good paying job in the off-season. I was fortunate because I had already begun a career with Aflac. Selling insurance, in particular Aflac, allowed me some financial peace; collecting renewals and helping people with their claims felt good to me. I enjoyed people, so working for Aflac was a natural for this Vandy grad, and I continued selling for thirty-plus more years and winning many sales awards; one day in the distant future I landed Wal-Mart for Aflac.

Finding an off-season job for 100 percent of the Minor League players was the key to financial survival. During the Minor League season, you would never make enough salary to satisfy your wants, much less your needs. Thus, it was important to find something that would not just support you during off-season from October through February but also allow you to build up a little savings.

The guys would head home after the last game of the season, and many would still live with parents. I knew many married teammates who lived with their parents with the understanding it was just for the four-and-a-half-month off-season. Thank God your family understood your financial conditions and supported you while you still chased your dreams.

For a ballplayer who has limited skills and no college education, the pickings were slim. So in baseball, we had construction workers, painters, grocery clerks, apprentices, roofers, dish washers, lawn care workers, and an occasional UPS driver. Being a UPS driver was the job many players wanted because it required no college education, it was mostly about physical ability, and most important, it paid better than any other job you could possibly obtain. In the month of December alone you could make enough to satisfy all your needs during the baseball season.

In later years I played with a guy named Dave Gumpert, and every day on the bus Gump talked about quitting baseball and going to work with UPS as a delivery guy. Once while we were on a road trip, a UPS brown truck pulled up beside the team charter, and Dave immediately rose to his feet, saluting the UPS vehicle and shouting at the top of his lungs, "UPS! UPS! UPS!"

The entire bus erupted with laughter, but Dave's point was well taken. It made veteran Minor League players on the dead-end street to nowhere take notice of their dire situation. They were on their way to becoming career Minor Leaguers, and the game of baseball had turned into a job. They were entering the crossroads of staying with the game or entering the Lunch Box League. Such was the financial picture for most of the Minor League players in Visalia, especially Rick Austin, affectionately known as "Wolfy."

☎

Richard Ray Austin, born August 5, 1959, in Baudett, Minnesota, was a piece of work and, to those who were fortunate to play Minor League baseball with him, a baseball legend. His reputation as a hard-nosed catcher, a team clown, and a real entrepreneur when it came to his creative ways to make money around the dugout was second to none. Fans of the game hear stories of players signing huge contracts and living the life of luxury. I tell you today, even a big league player looks back with a smile and fond memories on the stories lived in the Minor Leagues. Wolfy would provide those stories for all of us who played for Visalia in 1981.

As I look back at Wolfy, I still find it hard to believe some of the imaginative ideas he hatched to make money and survive in the Minor Leagues. He had no other choice. The previous season, he met a girl named Lynn in Wisconsin Rapids, or Whiskey Rapids, as the Twins players referred to it, and he relocated her to Visalia. It was hard enough for one player to live on $700 a month and impossible for two adults to financially make it.

Wolfy remained exceedingly thrifty during his entire baseball career. Even when he made it to Triple A Toledo, Ohio, for a season, he took a cooler on the bus and packed it with bread, peanut butter, bologna, condiments, and other staple items.

Tim Teufel told me he once asked Wolfy, "What is with the cooler?"

Wolfy replied, "Well, we are on an eight-day road trip, and this is all the food I will need for the trip iced down. No restaurants for me. I'm using my meal money to pay bills at home."

His penny-pinching was highly unlike any other player I ever played with. Wolfy was the ultimate frugal ballplayer.

Wolfy was all of five feet eleven inches and a buck eighty in weight. He was balding, yet possessed red hair all over his body, including his chest and shoulders. He was a scrapper on the field, had a great work ethic, and hustled as much as anyone. He made the most of his ability; he threw better than average, hit a little, but with no power, and also ran below average. Wolfy was a career Minor League player through and through! His natural baseball ability peaked in Single A ball, even though he caught his way to Triple A.

After a few conversations with Wolfy, you realized there was a better chance than not that he would never make the Dean's List in college. He was a simple guy, enjoying every day of life to the fullest, yet he had no backup plans after professional baseball. Wolfy's ability to look into the future stopped at the gates to the ballpark.

He was quite entertaining, he made all of us laugh with his Yogi Berraish comments, and most of the time the guys told him he was out of control. His looks and mannerisms would make you howl, and his comments made Forrest Gump seem like a Rhodes Scholar!

The first time Wolfy's creative genius sprang forth was in our Oaks dugout one day before a game. Walking in the dugout with a smile, he said out of the blue, "Hey, guys, how much will you give me to shave my entire body?"

The rest of us in the dugout raised our eyes toward the redheaded bear and just shook our heads in disbelief.

"No, I'm serious, guys! I'll shave all my hair off, pubes and all. How much is it worth? I could really use the cash!"

The team came up with about $45 to give Wolfy, and he put on a show for us immediately after the game. He went into the locker room showers and started shaving. He completed the task as he stood in front of the mirror; it looked like a freak show live from Bourbon Street. Wolfy didn't have a lick of hair on him and walked away totally content $45 richer, able to make ends meet one more week.

The next time Wolfy brought forth his latest ingenious way to pocket some cash involved his nasty habit of chewing tobacco. Professional baseball discourages chewing tobacco among players as a safety reason. Yes, it is true that chewing tobacco has been known to cause cancer, so it is probably a good idea. In actuality, probably a third of the players chew or dip something with a tobacco flavor, and baseball officials kind of turn their heads from these particular players' vice.

The commissioner's office has said its piece on the subject, so it is out of harm's way when it comes to a liability issue for future cancer occurrences. Besides, there are a lot of good players and exceptional managers who dip or chew, so let's just leave them alone and allow them to perform their jobs in professional baseball.

The Oaks had several players who chewed, and Wolfy was one of them. He entered the dugout with a new money-making idea. That day, he asked us, "Hey, how much you guys give me to drink this chewing tobacco juice?"

Instantly, a few guys responded, "Wolfy, you are a sick bastard!"

Well, Wolfy soon had the entire team agreeing to chip in some money to watch him take a red Solo plastic cup of tobacco juice he had been using and lift the cup to his lips. It was the most repulsive and sickening thing I had ever seen, and several players actually threw up in the dugout, me being one of them. I still gag just remembering the sight of the tobacco juice sliding out of the corners of Wolfy's mouth when he smiled at the guys in the dugout. We knew then that Wolfy would do just about anything to make money, and the $93 he pocketed drinking his tobacco juice surely wasn't enough.

☎

The all-time Wolfy story occurred during a road trip to Reno, Nevada. Remember earlier that I mentioned Reno was the players' favorite place to visit. We loved the bright lights and the cheap buffets. Players lived like kings in Reno, and it was the only place on the road that we ate steaks. The $9-per-day meal money went a long way there. That is, unless somebody asked you for money on the first day of a road trip. This time, Wolfy was not coming up with a scheme to make money. No, this time Wolfy wanted the team to pay for his wedding, which was to occur in Reno on the second day of the road trip.

The first night at the yard, Wolfy approached me before the game and asked to speak to me in private, "Hey, Scotti, I want to get married! You know I've been living with Lynn for a while, and I think it's time to get married. She has a good job working the drive-through line at Burger Chef, and we think we want to settle down in Visalia after the season."

I expressed congratulations and asked him when he planned on doing it.

Wolfy told me, "Tomorrow if possible." And then he dropped the bomb: "Hey, the problem is, I don't have any money to pay for it. I got a good deal at this place, the Chapel of the Bells. I can get a wedding, a real preacher, a marriage certificate, and a ride in a limo for thirty minutes for around $120. So, I was wondering if you could ask the team to help pay for it. You know, ask each guy to maybe kick in $5 or so."

I looked at Wolfy in total disbelief and asked, "Wolfy, you don't have any money to get married? Why would you even think about getting married?"

He responded with his well-thought-out vision for life, "Well, Lynn is in line for a management trainee position at Burger Chef, and that pays about $7 per hour."

Trying to reason with the team's jester was pointless, and I knew it was a bad idea to ask the guys to pay for the wedding. Since it was the first day of a six-day road trip, the additional $54 in meal money would be held close to each player's chest. It would have been easier to pull a bone away from a starving Doberman. Nevertheless, I promised Wolfy on the spot that I would ask the guys to chip in for the wedding.

First, I approached Skip. He rolled his eyes and said, "Oh, boy!" But he granted me permission to hold a team meeting to discuss the upcoming wedding plans.

The entire team gathered in right field. Wolfy was center stage along with me as I announced that he had decided to get married. Most of the guys congratulated him and spoke words of encouragement.

That is, until I dropped the grenade in the middle of the circle: "Hey, guys, Wolfy has asked for our help, and he wants me to ask all of you if you would help pay for his wedding here in Reno. He wants to get married tomorrow, and he is asking all of us to chip in $5 to help pay for the ceremony and limo ride."

"No f'ing way, man!"

"The hell with Wolfy."

It was a unanimous response. I had never seen a team so ada-mant about a "hell no!" After serious and intense negotiating, I convinced all of them to begrudgingly chip in $4 apiece to offset the matrimonial costs. Even Skip chipped in, but I collected only $96. That was $24 short.

Wolfy asked me, "What should I do?"

I advised, "If you can't come up with $24 for your wedding, you have no business getting married in the first place. Tell Lynn to work a double shift at Burger Chef."

But Wolfy entered into matrimony full steam ahead! He came

The wedding of Rick "Wolfy" Austin and Lynn.

into my room after the game and thanked me for helping get the guys to chip in. Then he started rummaging through my closet in search of wedding attire. "Hey, man, you and me are about the same size, and my clothes aren't so good. Do you think I could wear these pants of yours?"

The next morning he wore my pants and Jim Weaver's shirt as he walked down the aisle. He provided the wake-up call for every one of his teammates at 9:00 a.m. for his 9:30 wedding. The entire team walked next door and sat in the courtyard of the Chapel of the Bells. We were all tired from lack of sleep, yet the excitement of seeing Wolfy getting married on our dime kept us all on the edge of our seats. Oh, and one more point of interest, poor Wolfy somehow managed to step in dog poo on his way down the aisle.

Front row, left to right: Jimmy Christensen, Tony Pilla, and Ray Stein with the team in Reno.

The $120 wedding in Reno reminded me of the simple life we were living. It was a bare bones existence, making little money, yet playing baseball daily. The wedding in Reno broke the monotony of being just another road trip. We all left the ceremony smiling, and any baseball pressures we felt seemed to be a little lighter as we walked back to our rooms to get some needed sleep. Seeing Wolfy climb into the limo at 10:30 in the morning for his thirty-minute ride with his bride brought a smile of satisfaction to my face. I knew for all the Wolfys who played in Minor League baseball, it would never get any better than that!

Chapter 19

Let the Good Times Roll

We had some good times traveling to the California League cities. Our favorite, of course, was Reno. In addition to getting quality inexpensive meals almost anywhere in town, we could try our hands at blackjack at the $2 table. Most players walked up to the tables with $20 cash in their pockets, but it was $20 they could ill afford to lose.

On one trip to Reno, some of the Visalia Oaks players and I were playing blackjack at a table with Johnny Lee, not long after *Urban Cowboy* made him famous. I thought it so odd that here was the man whose hit song highlighted, "Looking for love in all the wrong places," and that was exactly what we were doing most of the time. He was a nice guy and stayed at the table with us for several hours. He invited us to be his guests at his show the next night, but we had to bow out due to our own show against the Reno Padres. The Oaks players who played cards at the blackjack table with Johnny Lee that one night in Reno went to see the movie *Urban Cowboy* the first chance we had on a day off.

We met football celebrities on a road trip to Stockton. After a celebrity softball game before our game in that city, many stars of the Oakland Raiders football team were hanging around the dugout. The Oaks players took pictures and obtained autographs of great players like Art Shell and Kenny King.

One of my favorite trips during the California League play was to Redwood City, home of the California Angels Single A club. There Hrbek and I met two pretty waitresses at a local restaurant.

Redwood City was about twenty-five miles from San Francisco

and twenty-five miles from San Jose. There was nothing special about the city or even the ballpark other than the texture of the grass. The grass at the park was the thickest and darkest green color you have ever seen, and you just loved lying on it during pregame calisthenics. The hotel was just around the corner from the yard.

Next to the hotel was a restaurant where the visiting team ate every meal. Herbie and I were in the restaurant one day, chatting with the local talent in the form of two blonde waitresses. As fate would have it, the next day's game was in the afternoon, which meant that players were free to enjoy the surroundings away from the park starting about 5:00 p.m. The two ladies were coincidentally off from work after the lunch shift.

The four twenty-year-olds decided to take the coeds' Volkswagen into San Francisco. It would be the first trip into the Bay City for Herbie and me, and we had plans to do it up right. We had just been paid, so both of us had an extra hundred dollars in our pockets. We offered to pay for the gas if the girls would drive. Besides, fuel for a Volkswagen was not that much, so the rest of the cash went for other more important things.

The six-foot four-inch Hrbek had to sit in the front seat, and I climbed in the back with the girl I considered the better looker of the two. We had a blast and drove all over San Francisco in the small punchbuggy, seeing the Fisherman's Wharf, driving Lombard Street, which is noted for being the crookedest street in the world, and stopping at Haight-Ashbury. Neither player had ever seen so many pipes, bongs, and tie-dyed shirts as we did at Haight-Ashbury. We had no idea this was the center of the 1960s hippie movement. Every person there could tell you the name of every Grateful Dead song ever written.

Later that evening we took the trolley, and that in itself proved to be a memorable experience. We had bought several six-packs of beer during the personal tour of the Golden Gate City and were running low before we got on the trolley. We hopped inside a local store, and I walked out with six tall Budweisers in a brown grocery bag, perfect for a trolley ride through the streets of San Francisco on a cool summer night. Strangely, there were no other passengers aboard, so we jumped right on and selected an outside seat. After paying the elderly black conductor, each of us whipped out a Budweiser and kicked back for the ride up and down the hills of San Francisco.

Within a flash, the conductor stopped the trolley and politely told the partygoers that we could not drink alcohol on public transportation. We were disappointed because our frolic included something to wet our whistles.

Since I didn't like to take no for an answer, I began explaining to the man, "Sir, we are a couple of Minor League ballplayers with our lady friends, and we have never been to San Francisco before. In fact this is our first trolley car ride, and this is the only thing I really wanted to do tonight. Can't you work with us? We promise to keep the drinks out of sight from public view."

The kind public employee, interested in young baseball players, replied, "Well, I certainly would like to welcome you to San Fran and I do like baseball, but I just don't want to lose my job letting young folks drink on my trolley car!"

As I listened intently to what the man was saying, I was especially attentive to his Louisiana accent. At just the right time before we walked away or the beer had to be tossed, I asked, "You sound as if you might be from back home, say, Louisiana?"

The man smiled and said, "Yes, sir, Baton Rouge!"

I knew exactly what to do in dealing with someone from Louisiana, especially Baton Rouge. This gentleman was most likely an LSU Tigers fan through and through. In a matter of seconds I bellowed out the "Tiger Rag": "Hold that Tiger. Hold that Tiger."

The conductor began to sing along, and the two of us acted as if we had just witnessed an LSU touchdown on a Saturday night. I told the man that I was recruited to play football at LSU, and the legendary coach Charlie "Mac" Alexander came to my house once to try and get me to play football for the Bengal Tigers.

I said, "While Coach Mac was visiting with me, Coach Paul 'Bear' Bryant called the house to speak with me and try to convince me to play football at Alabama.

"Coach Mac took the phone from this Pensacola recruit and spoke to Coach Bryant for twenty minutes.

"Coach Mac gave me the phone back, and Coach Bryant told me before he hung up: 'Don't believe anything that LSU coach tells you!'"

I knew a lot about LSU football, and it was one of my last football choices along with Alabama before selecting Vanderbilt.

The LSU fan laughed at our conversation, and the trolley remained parked for a while longer. Changing the conversation to Billy Cannon and Tommy Casanova took the man back in history to a time when his life was centered on football on a Saturday night in Baton Rouge. The fifty-year-old conductor reminisced to a moment years earlier when he worked concessions at Tiger Stadium. He talked about the championship season in 1959 and how Billy Cannon was the star.

The four young people listened intently to his recollection of the Tigers' golden days and almost wished we had been there to watch LSU beat Clemson in the Sugar Bowl 7–0 in 1959. That was all it took for the man to make an exception: "Okay, y'all climb aboard and try and keep your beers in a brown bag when you need a drink." He sang, "Hold that Tiger. Hold that Tiger," as he started the trolley on its regular course.

We jumped off to get four brown bags and even bought another six-pack as we rode up and down the Powell-Hyde trolley line. He never stopped to pick anyone else up, and the only stop of the night was at Aquatic Park near Ghirardelli Square. We rode from end to end several times until we consumed our drinks and only stopped because one waitress had to use the restroom. It was better than a good night, and it reinforced my idea that it was important to know a little something about everything, especially Southeastern Conference football. You never know when it will come in handy.

☎

One more memorable Minor League adventure has to be mentioned because it was so unique. It was 1983, and I was playing with the Albuquerque Dukes. We were on the road visiting the Edmonton Trappers. I liked playing in the Pacific Coast League (PCL) since they played in so many interesting cities and even traveled into Canada. They played in some great cities like Portland, Tucson, Oahu, Phoenix, as well as in Vancouver, British Columbia, and Edmonton, Alberta, Canada. In 1983 the sights and entertainment in the PCL were much better than in Amarillo, Modesto, Savannah, Montgomery, and Chattanooga—all places very familiar to me.

It was my first time to play the Edmonton team, and they had several players that I would meet down the road and befriend, such as pitchers Mickey Mahler and Bill Mooneyham. I thought it was interesting to be playing in Canada, and the Trappers coach oddly was named Moose Stubing.

Every day is the same in the life of a professional baseball player, at least with respect to knowing what day it is. A weekend day is no different from a weekday when it comes to pregame activities and game time. If you are a visitor, you get to the park around 4:00 p.m. for a 7:30 p.m. game, and this day, Paul Voigt and I arrived at the Edmonton Park a little bit earlier than was customary. It was a beautiful, sunny day for a 1:00 p.m. game in Alberta, and we walked on the field about 10:30 a.m.

Maybe it was just luck or maybe it was fate, but Paul and I are so glad, even to this day, that we walked on the field before anyone else from either team that Saturday in Edmonton. I began to converse with some local kids standing by the edge of the fence and asked them if they were on holiday, as foreigners often call it, or if they were skipping school. They looked at me with bewilderment and said, "We don't go to school on a Saturday!"

Maybe I didn't know what day of the week it was, but I did know who the Edmonton Oilers were. I needed to say something clever in order to look bigger than life in my Dukes uniform. My knowledge about hockey was limited, other than I watched the playoffs and could tell when the team scored. I couldn't understand why there were three periods compared to the customary four in football and basketball, and "off sides" calls still befuddled me. I did know who Bobby Hull, Phil Esposito, and Bobby Orr were, and I had heard of "The Great One," Wayne Gretzky.

Wayne Gretzky without question is the greatest hockey player to ever live. He would get at least one vote from anyone who could vote that he was second to none in overall performance. He was the leading scorer in NHL history and had more than two hundred goals four seasons in a row. In comparison, it would be like a baseball player hitting eighty home runs a year for four consecutive seasons. When he retired in 1999, he held forty regular-season records, fifteen playoff records, and six All-Star records. He was on the other side of great as far as hockey fans were concerned, and I was familiar with his notoriety after just his second season in the game.

Doing my best to appear smart, I mentioned the Oilers' Great One with the kids. The Oilers were in the playoffs, and Gretzky was the perfect lead for recovery in the conversation. While the kids and I were talking, Paul Voigt was walking up to the fence. Paul was from Long Island, New York, and a huge Islanders fan. The Islanders were dominating the league during this time and had their own superstars like Billy Smith, Brent and Duane Sutter, Denis Potvin, Mike Bossy, and Bryan Trottier.

The schoolkids said, "Yeah, Gretzky, he's the greatest. He's sitting right over there." They pointed to a man sitting alone about ten bleachers up on the third base side.

Pauly and I looked at each other and, without saying a word, proceeded to walk into the stands. Our metal cleats made a clanging noise of metal on metal, but we didn't care.

Wayne Gretzky could not have been nicer to the two Minor League players, and all he wanted to do was to talk baseball. He told us he loved coming to the park, and if he wasn't playing hockey now, he would have wanted to be a Major League shortstop. Both of us sat with the twenty-two-year-old blond-headed superstar and took it all in. There was not a nicer professional athlete we would ever meet, and Gretzky was a gentleman even in his early twenties. He genuinely acted concerned for our careers and took an interest in our backgrounds as well.

Here we were trying to get to the big leagues, and we were talking to someone who would one day become the greatest player in his profession. Pauly was smart enough not to rub it in that the Islanders were dominating the league and would probably beat the Oilers in the playoffs, which they eventually did. Both of us were fans of great athletes and even bigger fans of classy guys, so we really appreciated Gretzky's time.

Before we walked back to the field, Gretzky asked if we wanted to come to a Stanley Cup finals match the following day. "Heck yeah," we said at the same time. Gretzky had a couple of assists, and it was one of the most exciting sporting events I had ever attended. We sat center ice, just above the bench. Hockey is a fast-moving sport, the complete opposite of baseball. I thought, *Why in the world would Wayne Gretzky want to be a baseball player?*

Imagine being a baseball fan who loves baseball more than any other sport and you are about to attend a World Series game. Imagine walking up to the players' ticket window and asking the ticket attendant, "Excuse me, my name is Scotti Madison, and Babe Ruth has left me and my friend two tickets to the World Series game tonight!" Would that not be a story you would remember the rest of your life? That was exactly what transpired the night we were on Wayne Gretzky's pass list. Pauly was a veteran of hockey matches, and it was his greatest moment at a hockey match. My first hockey match was during the Stanley Cup finals, and I was the guest of the greatest hockey player of all time. For me, it would be downhill attending hockey matches from that point onward. Wayne later sent each of us an autographed photo.

I have told this story to numerous hockey fans over the years, and they look at me with skepticism: *Really, first match, greatest player?* Other than a handful of Albuquerque Dukes players, only Paul Voigt, my best friend in baseball, can vouch for this Forrest Gump–like tale! Maybe Wayne Gretzky remembers it too.

The Great One, Wayne Gretzky.

Chapter 20

Salt of the Earth

The life of a young Minor League player can be quite lonesome, especially when he often plays so far from home. The California League could not have been much farther away from my home near Pensacola, Florida. My family couldn't afford to come out to California for a visit, as was the case for the majority of players on the Oaks team that season. The importance of finding family and being able to connect with local folks was critical in the emotional well-being of young ballplayers. Too many destructive vices followed ballplayers around, and we desperately needed to surround ourselves with people of character. We needed to have small groups of accountable folks to break bread with and pray with, providing encouragement when life's problems became overwhelming. Amos 5:4 reminds us: "Seek Me [God] that you may live."

Minor League players needed to seek something other than pleasure, and I had been as guilty as any. Many of us weren't living in Visalia with an outlook toward eternity for sure. And the kind of living we were actually doing would eventually cause a few of us problems later in life with addictive behaviors. Like too many young people today, we were living for the moment, and the most important person to each of us was himself.

The first place a player should have looked to find true love, hope, and encouragement away from the yard was the local church. Since the Oaks Sunday games were often in the evenings, players had time to get up and go to church if they so chose. Most of us didn't so choose, and we needed prodding from a couple of faith-led players. The one consistent player who was always inviting players to church was Jay Pettibone. I liked having Jay on the team because he was a solid, soft-speaking guy, who lived his life for God. I don't think there was a selfish bone in his body.

Jay was a real workhorse on the pitching staff and battled the opposition every game, ending the 1981 season with an impressive 14–8 record. Jay was not a bonus baby and had been drafted the 743rd pick out of the 30th round. He had been released by the Rangers a year earlier and was picked up as a free agent by the Twins. Pettibone was a good find for the Twins and was a better find for all the guys on the Oaks team. Jay was a veteran in life's experiences compared to the other players. He had already faced baseball hardships as a released player, so he was more seasoned than most of us. He had a more mature, a more realistic outlook toward baseball and life than I did.

Jay was what a southerner would refer to as "the salt of the earth." Thus, he was the team's spiritual leader, and I imagine that during that season, he reached out to everyone on the team at least one time, offering something everlasting. I went to church with Jay and pitcher Sam Arrington on some Sundays at the Church of Christ in Tulare, and the church often hosted a Sunday dinner after the service. Getting some home-cooked food was always special and helped create the feeling of being with family.

Besides attending church, the feeling of family occurred when local fans came to the games and befriended Oaks players, inviting us to their homes for a meal or providing a place to escape from those drab apartments we lived in.

I hit the jackpot and was fortunate to find a real family that I truly loved like my own while playing in Visalia. A local family who had taken several of us in as second sons during our stay in Visalia was the Greens. Jay Green was the father; there may not have been a nicer man who ever lived in the San Joaquin Valley. Mary was his devoted wife and a passionate Dodgers fan. She had the disposition to be everyone's mother, and she became the "mom" for many of us, so many miles away from our real homes.

Jay worked for Farmers Insurance Group, and his offices were located on Tulare Avenue in Visalia. He won every sales award that Farmers created, and I wouldn't be surprised if they eventually named an award after him. He was a natural salesperson, and he had an innate ability to relate to people, get them to laugh and open up to him. Every now and then he would call me "sucker" with a high-pitched voice, followed by a bellow of a laugh. Soon to follow after his laugh were a couple of coughs, due to years of smoking earlier in his life. The couple welcomed me in their home any day I wanted to stop by and visit.

Weekends were special because Jay grilled out, and Jim Weaver and I sat around the pool and relaxed before a game. In the background, we could hear Vin Scully on the radio broadcasting the Dodgers' Saturday afternoon game throughout the house on three radios for Mary.

Scotti with Jay Green, September 1987, Oakland.

On all days off and after most games, I ended up at the Greens'
house and just sat around and talked with Jay. He would go to the
keg he kept iced down and bring me a frosty mug filled to the brim.
He was another salt-of-the-earth man, a mentor for me.

This Oaks catcher picked his brain daily about insurance and
selling. I was already licensed with Aflac out of Columbus, Georgia
(it was called American Family Life Assurance in 1981). Jay had
never heard of American Family Life Assurance and tried to convince me to sell for Farmers Insurance. He just wanted to help me
and saw great potential in sales for this Vanderbilt graduate. The
two of us remained friends, and Jay and Mary often visited me in
San Francisco or Oakland when I came back to play within driving
distance of Visalia.

Scotti and Mary Green, September 1987.

Chapter 21

I've Seen Almost Everything

Noteworthy happenings occurred in the Minor Leagues during my travels around the country.

I saw a man in Nashville, Tennessee, pass out while trying to play a high note on a trumpet for the national anthem.

I participated in a cow-milking contest before a game in Louisville, Kentucky, and won.

I saw my share of streakers run across old War Memorial Stadium in Buffalo, New York, totally buck naked.

I watched a Mexican win $100 in a jalapeño-eating contest in San Antonio, Texas, consuming eighty-seven jalapeños in five minutes, a feat that ultimately sent him to the hospital.

I saw a man named Hook Slide run and slide over a popcorn box placed on concrete again and again in Little Rock, Arkansas, just to make beer money.

☎

Yet one of the craziest things happened while I was playing for the hometown Visalia Oaks. I had an epileptic attack in the on-deck circle, or at least that's what everyone who saw it thought was taking place!

It was a normal summer night in Visalia, in the high seventies with zero chance of rain. The stadium lights always attracted an abundance of bugs, and more bugs than normal seemed to be flying around. During the entire game, we swatted at moths to keep them away from our faces.

Jim Weaver had entered the batter's box, and I was on deck. One persistent moth kept annoying me, and I kept batting it away. For some reason the moth entered the right ear hole of my helmet, but it didn't stop there. It kept going and ventured all the way into my ear.

Weaver had just picked up a base hit and was standing on first base when all eyes moved back across the field to the on-deck circle. There the crowd witnessed me shaking violently and repeatedly striking the right side of my head. Then I began to roll around on the ground. The moth kept fluttering in my ear, driving me absolutely insane.

It appeared that I was a man possessed. I would stand up and act normal, then the moth would vibrate against my eardrum, and I would shake my head as fast as I could shake it. Then I would roll around on the ground like a catfish out of water.

Finally, the trainer hollered, "He's having an epileptic attack. Hurry!"

That prompted the trainer and two players to try and hold me down while they stuck a tongue depressor in my mouth.

After I bit the first tongue depressor in half, I shouted, "It's a moth in my ear! There's a moth in my ear!"

The game was delayed as they lifted me to my feet and took me to the Oaks dugout. They first stuck a flashlight in my ear canal, hoping that would draw the moth out. That didn't work, so they blew air in it and followed that up with water, trying to drown the culprit. Nothing worked, and nothing gave me any relief. I kept shaking my head violently and saying, "This is driving me crazy."

At last Manager Dick Phillips told the trainer, "For God's sake, take this guy to the emergency room before he goes insane!"

I shook all the way to the hospital, and my outlandish movements in the emergency room prompted most of the ER patients to look my way and keep a safe distance from the crazy man.

After a few tries the ER doctor removed the moth. The moth must have been a tough sucker; it was still alive, even after all those efforts to kill it.

Oddly enough, the next day, no one said a word to me about

the moth incident as I entered the locker room. That is, not until I walked on the field for pregame calisthenics. I was a little late on the field postmoth, and all the other guys had already started warm-ups when I reached the large circle of players.

As soon as I stood beside everyone, the entire team started flapping their arms, shaking their bodies and heads, and rolling around on the ground. A loud murmur came from the group as the entire team laughingly made the sound of a moth fluttering. I provided the guys with free entertainment for a couple of days after the moth attack!

☎

I had another significant run-in with an insect in my Minor League career. It happened in the dugout at Saint Mary's College field, home field of the San Antonio Dodgers. Manager Don LeJohn gave me the night off from play, telling me to take it easy and give my shoulder some rest.

The Dodgers players knew Manager LeJohn as "Ducky." As a player, he had a better than average Major League career, especially when you get an at bat in the World Series like Ducky did in 1965. He was called up after hitting .395 at Albuquerque as a player-coach in his twelfth year in the Minors. I always have had great respect for any former player who paid Minor League dues for five years or longer, so I liked LeJohn. Ducky was a thirty-one-year-old rookie when he struck his first two singles in his first two Major League at bats. He got one at bat in the World Series as a pinch hitter. Yet what his San Antonio players remembered most about Ducky was his cigarette smoking.

The San Antonio Dodgers took some of the most dreadful bus trips you could ever travel in the Minor Leagues. We took buses to El Paso, Little Rock, Tulsa, and across Texas to Midland, Amarillo, and Beaumont. It was customary for managers to sit in one of the first seats on the bus, right next to Bussie. But Ducky had a bad smoking problem, and he couldn't go any time without firing up a heater, even if it was in between innings. Thus, he sat in the very back of the bus, next to the bathroom, and smoked cigarettes all night long on a bus trip across Texas.

A player could look down the aisle in the pitch-black darkness and see a red light coming from the lighted end of Ducky's cigarette. You could watch the red flame move up and down from his knee to his lips all night long until the bus pulled up to the hotel in the early morning hours.

About the fifth inning the night I had off from play, I felt a stinging on my right knee. I couldn't figure out what happened to create such a sharp pain since I was just sitting there. The pain in my knee turned to a burning, tingling, and then numbing sensation.

Some two innings later a player saw a scorpion on the bench and a well-aimed bat crushed its head. After the game, I approached Charlie Strasser, the trainer, and told him my knee really hurt. Could the scorpion have bitten me? Charlie couldn't make out anything at the time of his examination so he gave me some aspirin and sent me home, saying, "Let's see how your knee feels in the morning." The next day was a getaway day, and the team was traveling to Beaumont, the shortest of the road trips.

By 8:30 the next morning, I couldn't move my entire right leg. It was as if the great orthopedic surgeon Phil Langer had just performed a total knee replacement on me. The pain was unbearable, and I had to practically crawl to the training room to show Charlie my infected limb. By then I had a hard time talking because my tongue was getting thicker and my vision was becoming blurry.

As the Dodgers bus pulled away for Beaumont, I was being admitted to a San Antonio hospital. Four days later I was released after being treated for a staph infection. It was another one of those times when adversity rears its ugly head. The odds of something like that happening were slim. Depending on the literature you read, only about twenty-five to forty of the approximately two thousand species of scorpions have toxins or venoms that are dangerous to humans. I hit the lottery when it came to the scorpion sting in San Antonio. It was just another minor setback in the Minor Leagues of life!

Oaks dugout, 1981 season, left to right: Jim Weaver, Lee Belanger, Rick Kyzer, Jay Pettibone, and Kevin Williams.

Chapter 22
Every Boy Wants a Baseball Card

B ack in Visalia, sometime during the summer of 1981, a representative of Topps baseball cards frequented the Visalia Oaks locker room. His sole purpose was to talk to every player and sign every player for the Topps Company. He was a big fellow, probably in his late sixties, and Skip Phillips knew him from years past. Skip treated him like royalty, welcoming him for a long conversation in the manager's office.

The man walked around to everyone's locker with a pen and Topps contracts in hand. He talked baseball, of course, and the rumor soon circulated around the clubhouse that he actually had known Babe Ruth. That added to his credibility, and the players were anxious to sign on the dotted line with Topps, no questions asked.

But when the former baseball player, and by now Babe Ruth's roommate, approached me, it was a different story. I looked at this large man, probably a first baseman back in the day, and told him I wouldn't sign the baseball card contract. This Topps representative had been signing players to Topps contracts for thirty years and never had a player turn him down.

He couldn't have known that just two days earlier, I had frequented the Modesto Public Library to finish my taxes. The team bus dropped me off at the front door after an afternoon game, and while I was there, I came across an article in the *Wall Street Journal* that addressed the efforts of two new baseball card companies entering the market to compete with Topps. The writer for the *WSJ* discussed the history of the sports cards companies going back to 1960, involving mainly three, Donruss, Fleer, and Topps.

Here is a summary of what I read:

In 1964 when Philadelphia Gum secured the rights for National

Football League cards, Topps simultaneously took over the American Football League. That left the Fleer Corporation with no product in either baseball or football.

Fleer then supported a legal complaint filed against Topps by the Federal Trade Commission (FTC). The complaint focused on the baseball card market, alleging that Topps was engaging in unfair competition through its aggregation of exclusive contracts. Such was the case in Visalia if you were to actually read the contract the company wanted each player to sign. It basically stated that Topps owned the rights to any marketing and advertising regarding a player's image, including movie rights. That language was always in the Topps contract, yet not one player took the time to look over it, except me!

Topps representatives talked to the guys when they were young and naïve and when the only thing of importance was getting their own baseball cards. Topps relied on the cool factor and used ego to suck every young player into signing on the dotted line.

To understand the issue even further, you need to know that a hearing examiner ruled against Topps in 1965, but the FTC reversed this decision on appeal. The commission concluded that because the contracts covered only the sale of cards with gum, competition was still possible by selling cards with other small, low-cost products. However, Fleer chose not to pursue such options and instead sold its remaining player contracts to Topps for $395,000 in 1966. The decision gave Topps an effective monopoly of the baseball card market.

In 1968 Fleer was approached by the Major League Baseball Players Association (MLBPA), the newly organized players' union, regarding a license to produce cards. The MLBPA was in a dispute with Topps over player contracts and offered Fleer the exclusive rights to market cards of most players starting in 1973, when a large number of Topps' contracts would expire. Fleer declined the proposal, not recognizing the value of such an offer by the MLBPA.

Fleer returned to the union in September 1974 with a proposal to sell new five-by-seven-inch satin patches of Major League players. By then, the MLBPA had settled its differences with Topps and reached an agreement that gave Topps a right of first refusal on such offers. Topps declined the offer, seeing no value in the new product. The union also rejected the proposal and sided with Topps, fearing that Fleer would cut into existing royalties from Topps sales, thus financially hurting the players.

In April 1975, Fleer asked for Topps to waive its exclusive rights and allow Fleer to produce a variety of small items featuring active baseball players. Topps refused, and Fleer then sued both Topps and the MLBPA to break the Topps monopoly. After several years of litigation, the court ordered the MLBPA to offer group licenses for baseball cards to companies other than Topps. Fleer and Donruss were thus allowed to begin making cards in 1981. This court decision would be overturned in the future, but as for the summer of 1981 when Herbie and I played for the Visalia Oaks, it was alive and well.

Topps was now facing competition, and I just happened to be at the right place at the right time to read those facts in the *WSJ* article. The representative for Topps tattled on me, so Skip Phillips called me into his office to discuss this Topps card disagreement.

Skip asked me in front of the Topps man, "What is your problem with this contract? Why won't you sign the contract?"

I proceeded to present Skip with a dissertation on the evil empire of the Topps Company, beginning with its exclusivity clauses in player contracts all the way to its monopoly in the baseball card market. Yet I ended by presenting Skip with hope, since two new companies were entering the card market: Donruss and Fleer. I ended my impromptu presentation by saying, "Competition is the American way to excellence."

Skip sat in silence, staring at me, and then pointed at me as he caught the eye of the Topps man. "Vanderbilt!" he proclaimed. Skip shrugged his shoulders and directly asked his friend from Topps, "Well, is this true?"

In fairness to the gentleman, he didn't know anything about what I was talking about; he was caught with his pants down.

Skip told his friend, "If I had known this, I wouldn't have signed this contract either! Scotti, go on back to your locker."

I was the only player not to sign that day in both clubhouses. In fact, only one other player and I never signed with Topps while playing in the Major Leagues. Fast-forwarding to 1987, I would meet Neal Heaton, the other nonconformist.

☎

To get to the end of my Topps story, we have to move ahead to the spring of 1987 when I had a phone call from the one and only Sy Berger. To fully appreciate just how serious Topps regarded this matter, you have to be aware of who Sy Berger is and why Topps called in the "Topps Guns" to settle my signing boycott.

Sy Berger is known as the father of the modern-day baseball card. He started out as a fixture in Major League locker rooms in the 1950s and 1960s, signing players to exclusive contracts for a measly $125. For the Visalia Oaks players the money had jumped up to a token $500, if you made it to the show, so it was still about your own card being a symbol of status.

It was in the fall of 1951 that the then twenty-eight-year-old Berger designed the 1952 Topps baseball card set, sitting at his kitchen table on Alabama Avenue in Brooklyn, New York. The card design he created then still provides the same look and feel on the modern-day card. Sy would eventually work for Topps for fifty years, and this day in 1987, he was handling what he told me was a media faux pas for Topps.

Before I could respond to him, the Brooklyn native addressed the problem head-on, "We got a problem! You are one of two players to ever play in the Major Leagues that Topps has not signed to a contract. This makes us look bad. What is it going to take for you to sign with us?"

Sy's comments caught me completely by surprise. I was not expecting a phone call about Topps baseball cards. Thus, I had no immediate answer to Mr. Berger's question.

He told me that the Royals and the Expos were playing a spring game the next week in West Palm Beach, and he would personally come down from New York to talk with me and Neal Heaton, the other scoundrel in the pot.

The meeting was agreed upon, and I looked forward to meeting Neal for the first time. While playing for the Miami Hurricanes, he happened to be selected to the 1980 Collegiate All-America team that I made while playing at Vanderbilt. In fact, Neal had the distinction of making it two years in a row.

The day soon came when Neal and I met in the outfield. You would have thought we had been personally acquainted for years, yet it was our All-Star selection in college that cemented the conversation. The brief introduction turned quickly to the business at hand.

Neal asked me, "Well, what do you want to do? Do you want to sign with these guys?"

Before Sy garnered our attention, Neal and I were in harmony on the following: we would agree to one baseball card (later Neal gave in on that); we would select the photo we wanted to use for our cards; we would receive two hundred of our baseball cards to distribute; and we would sign for a $5,000 bonus, not $500. These requests were certainly in line with the unique situation and with the desperate situation that Sy faced to get us signed.

Sy walked on the field that day, and the three of us came to an agreement and finalized our business on the left field foul line before the Expos and the Royals played.

I never spoke to Neal Heaton again and had only one more conversation with Sy Berger, regarding the photo I selected for my one and only baseball card, 1988 Topps Trader Set, #63T.

Chapter 23

Just Play Me Anywhere

E very game I played in the Twins organization, I took the field as either a catcher or a designated hitter (DH). I hated being the DH. My impatience and hyperactive mannerisms were not well-suited characteristics for sitting in a dugout and waiting for a turn to bat, which occurred maybe once every forty-five minutes. I liked to play and wanted to play any position in the field as long as I was able to get an at bat.

I started playing shortstop as a kid and played in the middle infield all the way to college. It was at Vanderbilt where I started my freshman season as a third baseman, later playing right field and then becoming a catcher my junior and senior seasons. I was told in college, even as an All-SEC right fielder, that if you can become a catcher as a switch-hitter, you can make it to the big leagues.

So at the end of my sophomore season, I played in the Alaska Summer League, and I caught batting practice every day for Mark Newman and Rich Hacker of the 1978 Kenai Peninsula Oilers. I taught myself how to catch, painfully, every day, exhausting myself before I played in the real game for the Kenai team. I also volunteered to warm up pitchers in between starts in order to obtain extra work behind the plate.

I felt it was important to make myself available to play any position that a team might need a man who could hit a little bit. One time in the summer of 1984, while I was playing for the Birmingham Barons, Manager Roy Majtyka played me at every position in a game except pitcher, shortstop, and center field. In a nine-inning game I played six different positions, and this occurred in Columbus, Georgia, in front of all my friends and colleagues at Aflac, friends like Tom Giddens, Jim Thompson, Penny Pennington, and Frank Land.

Playing behind the plate as catcher, the quarterback of the baseball team, was my favorite position on the field. Since I was drafted as a catcher, that was the pigeonhole where I was stuck while playing for the Twins and later the Dodgers. It took my sale to the Detroit Tigers to finally open the door for me to play other positions on defense in professional baseball.

After my sale to the Tigers for the aforementioned miniscule amount of cash, $10,000 to be exact, my willingness to field ground balls at first base on my first day in the Tigers spring camp led to

The catcher with umpires, caught out of uniform; their luggage was lost.

my later being referred to as a utility player. Like every player who joins a new organization, you want to do everything you can to make a good impression. Thus, as soon as I stepped on the field, I decided to help out the shortstop, Venezuelan Pedro Chavez, who was fielding ground balls from a coach.

Chavez wanted to make some throws across the diamond to first base, so this new Tiger player stepped in as a first baseman. I reached into my bag of tricks, the Worth catching bag that contained everything that Monty Hall on *Let's Make a Deal* could ask for. Today I pulled out a first base mitt.

I stepped on first base and took throw after throw from Chavez, and soon the second baseman, Gary Springer, was tossing balls my way. After both middle infielders had their fill, I stepped off the bag, and a coach began to hit some ground balls to me at first. It certainly helped that I was once a shortstop and a third baseman, so my fielding was quite acceptable. I was no Kent Hrbek in defensive prowess, but I held my own quite well for several years into the future every time I got a chance to play at first.

After twenty or so ground balls into the day, Minor League Field Director Frank Franchi approached me. He came out to first base with quite a smile on his face and with his hand extended. From day one, I knew the career Minor League player and lifetime coach would always be truthful with me.

That day Frank questioned my playing first base, "Hey, Scotti, Frank Franchi, Minor League Field Director. I see you fielding some ground balls at first base. I know we acquired you as a catcher. We didn't know you also played some first! When was the last time you played first base?"

Was Frank asking me when was the last time I played first base in professional baseball, or was he asking when I last played first? I chose to answer the latter question and told him I played first base last year. There was a lot of truth in my response because I had played first base for my church softball team in the fall of 1983. Yeah, maybe Frank was referring to a stint at first base in professional baseball, but he should have been a little more direct in his question. I then proudly told Frank I had played some third base in the same league.

Frank shook his head with a hint of satisfaction and said, "Well, we didn't have any record of that, so this is a bonus for our organization." That ended the conversation, and Frank walked away.

I found myself starting at first base the very next day in an inner squad game. I was out of place most of the day playing defense and embarrassingly missed being the cutoff man on a throw to home plate by the center fielder. I did pick up two hits, and that softened my mental deficiency on defense for the powers that be; they were mental mistakes I would never make again at first in either the Minors or the Majors.

☎

It seemed puzzling to me that the Tigers really didn't know what defensive positions I was capable of playing. I had to wonder, How much effort really goes into determining the best place to play an athlete within a Major League organization? Are you pigeonholed into one set position at the draft, and it is out of the ordinary for you to find another position more suitable to your talents and more advantageous to the organization? Is it often just left up to chance? I had witnessed several ballplayers throughout the years perform admirably at a different defensive position in the field, often totally baffling baseball management. When that happened, someone in management took credit for it as if it was a stroke of genius, when it more than likely occurred due to sheer luck and player determination. A player might be drafted as an outfielder, and an organization would find out by happenstance that he was better suited playing another position.

The most obvious example of position change occurred while I was playing for the Kenai Peninsula Oilers in Alaska, the summer of 1978. It involved Dave Stieb, the great pitcher for the Toronto Blue Jays who pitched for sixteen seasons and played in seven All-

Star games. Dave was the center fielder for the Kenai Oilers until he fortuitously pitched in front of one particular Blue Jays scout. No matter what other story you hear about Dave Stieb's becoming a Blue Jays pitcher, this one is the gospel truth.

The Peninsula Oilers that year were one of four teams in the league, and we traveled by air to play our opponents in Anchorage, Fairbanks, and Palmer. By car, the trip to Anchorage from Kenai was more than three hours, but as the crow flies, it was a thirty-five-minute flight to play the Anchorage Pilots. We flew Alaska Aeronautical Industries, which we appropriately named "aai do or die," due to the incredibly rough flights we took on a weekly basis. From there the Oilers had to drive forty-five minutes to play Palmer, and we played in this Matanuska Valley borough.

Palmer was known back then and is still famous for growing ridiculously large vegetables; we saw cabbages bigger than pumpkins the summer of 1978; some were upwards of seventy pounds. The summer temperature was rather cool, and the temperature averaged in the high sixties during July. The vegetables seemed to adapt to the cool summer temperatures, and the many insect pests, diseases, and weeds that are common in the lower forty-eight are not common in Alaska. The biggest difference in crop growth was the amount of sunlight. It never seemed to get dark when we played there. In June, for instance, Palmer gets nineteen hours of sunlight every day. This sunlight catapulted Palmer to be the world record holder in size for kale, kohlrabi, rutabagas, Romanesco broccoli, turnips, and green and purple cabbages.

That it was cooler than normal and there was light until midnight are also pertinent to this story about Dave Stieb pitching on a fluke in our game against the Palmer team. The season had been in play for almost a month, and several Oilers players were earlier drafted in the June draft of 1978. Major League organizations sent their scouts to the Alaska Summer League to view the wealth of talent, and many were also hanging around to try and sign the unsigned draft picks.

Stieb was drafted in the fifth round of the amateur draft and, in discussions with the Toronto Blue Jays, was asking for $25,000. The Blue Jays were offering him a bonus of $12,000, so they were far apart, and he was one of the unsigned players the Blue Jays scout was hustling to get a signed contract before Stieb gave up on Toronto's offer and headed back to Southern Illinois.

☎

None of us were sleeping that well, especially players who were playing in Alaska for the first time. It was difficult at best to get accustomed to the lengthy daylight in Alaska. Even when it was supposedly dark, a haze of light remained constant. It never appeared coal mine dark, not even for just one day during the summer months. In fact, we played one game with the Fairbanks team that started at midnight and was advertised as the longest day of the year in Alaska.

I was among those having serious sleeping problems because it never seemed dark enough in my bedroom. I put towels and aluminum foil around the curtains in an attempt to block out the incessant light coming in the windows.

When the team traveled to Palmer in 1978, there were no hotels to speak of, and the players and coaches slept in the basement of the local high school gymnasium. We entered through the basketball gym and walked across the gym floor to a back stairwell that led to the basement. This area served as the locker room for the physical education department and reeked of stale jockey straps. The Palmer staff had set up army-looking cots for the visiting teams and had sprinkled the entire locker room with cots pointing in every direction. We obviously complained about the sleeping conditions at first glance, and our concerns elevated once we took our initial showers in mountain-fed cold water, located at the far end of the locker room.

What the entire team overlooked was the wonderful fact that we were sleeping in a basement; there were no windows. We didn't recognize this blessing until it was too late the next day! The switch for the lighting in the room was located at the entrance to the stairwell, which was our only escape to the outside world. The room would remain illuminated until midnight. That was the "lights out" time our coaches Mark Newman and Rich Hacker set for the team in Palmer.

In his baseball future, Mark continued to coach college baseball until he joined the Yankees in 1989 and served as a top executive earning the title of senior vice president of baseball operations. Rich Hacker befriended Mark due to their SIU ties, and Rich would coach for the Cardinals and Blue Jays big league teams. His coaching career ended after a serious car accident on Martin Luther King Bridge in St. Louis in July 1993 that forced him to retire.

With curfew set for midnight, after the late afternoon game, the entire team, including players and coaches, trooped into the only local restaurant and bar in town. It was situated across the street from the Palmer Welcome Station, which was the store where I bought the white timber wolf hide I sent to country star Jerry Reed. The pool hall was a good place for a hamburger and cold beer, and the pool tables were better than adequate. The floor had scattered sawdust on it, and the dim lighting throughout the room made the establishment appear to be the setting for the miners' merriment in the Klondike gold rush of 1897. After every pool shot, I expected to hear Jack London read a few lines from *The Call of the Wild*.

All of us left the bar about the same time, and we stumbled back to the Palmer High School gymnasium. About 11:55, everyone had dressed for bed, brushed our teeth, and anticipated the lights going dark shortly. Mark and "Hack," as we affectionately called Rich, continued to talk, as did the players for a while longer. Mark Newman jumped up, stroked the light switch, and the room went dark about 1:00 a.m. Even though the smells coming out of the lockers were unpleasant and the snoring was bothersome, it was pleasantly cool, perfect for sleeping, and it was the darkest room we had seen in almost a month. It turned out to be the best night of rest for the whole team during that summer.

Our sleep was so deep that the first sound we heard the following morning was Coach Mark Newman shouting, "Oh, shit! I can't believe this! We overslept and missed the game today!"

Yes, we missed the game. We couldn't do anything about it then, so we just blew off the game, and the two teams scheduled a doubleheader for the next afternoon.

☎

The third day in Palmer, we fell way behind during the first game of the doubleheader. We fell so far behind that the coaches didn't want to waste any of our regular pitchers' arms in a losing cause, especially since we had one more game to play the same day. We had pitchers like Mark Ross from Texas A&M (a friend of the balloon-throwing Brian Little), Allan Ramirez from Rice University, and Atlee Hammaker from East Tennessee State University. All of these pitchers would pitch in the Major Leagues.

Since Palmer players were relentlessly running across home plate in the first game, Mark Newman walked to the mound and motioned for Dave Stieb to leave his center field position and come to the pitching mound. Newman was the pitching coach for the Southern Illinois Salukis, and he had two players on the Oilers team, shortstop Jerry DeSimone and Dave Stieb. Those three folks were the only three members of the Kenai baseball club who had any idea about Dave Stieb's pitching abilities on the mound. Stieb's first pitch in warm-ups sailed over the catcher's head and hit the backstop. From that point on it was lights out for the Palmer squad. Dave Stieb faced a total of nine batters that day, and I think he struck out eight of them.

The last we saw of the Blue Jays scout, he was running to the nearest pay phone to call Toronto and tell the Blue Jays to give Dave Stieb his $25,000. Dave would leave Alaska in a few days to join the

Toronto organization, and he soon became one of the best pitchers in Major League baseball for a long time. And there he was, starting out at first as a better than average prospect playing center field and later transitioning into a Major League All-Star pitcher by showing his wares at the right time and the right place.

Chapter 24

Herbie's Good-Bye

Sunday, August 23, 1981, in Visalia would start no differently than any other Sunday during our summer season. We had plans that day to eat lunch with the Greens and lie around the pool until we had to report to the yard. I rode with Lee Belanger and Jim Weaver to the park that day as I often did. Lee had a 1973 Gold 240Z, which was his prize possession. Lee was another Twins bonus baby like me and had signed for the whopping amount of $7,000. Lee originally asked for $10,000, and the representative of the Twins walked out of Lee's house in disgust. Lee took the $7,000, hoping it would last a few seasons, but it went only as far as a new car. Even though the 240Z was sporty looking, it certainly was not roomy, so either Jim or I sat in the very back all scrunched up for the fifteen-minute ride to Recreation Park.

There were just two weeks left in the season, and all year long, the Oaks had kicked ass in the California League. We ran away with the regular season, winning both halves, but we were required to have a playoff with some other team, and it was looking as if it might be the Lodi Dodgers. We would actually be playing the Dodgers on this Sunday evening, so it would give us a chance to size up our yearlong nemesis.

The Dodgers had some good players too! Guys like Dann Bilardello, Stu Pederson, Tony Brewer, and left-handed pitcher Tom Klawitter were well coached by their manager, Terry Collins. In the upcoming weeks the two teams would meet for the title game, and the Dodgers would beat the Oaks in a best-of-five game series. It would go down to the last game, and the Dodgers would win it in the ninth inning of play by hitting their last of five solo home runs, to win the championship game 5–4.

Oaks too much for Modesto in hitters' night at Del Webb

The Modesto A's couldn't be accused of lacking offensive punch Thursday night at Del Webb Field.

It wasn't nearly enough, however, as the Visalia Oaks romped to a 15-8 California League laugher.

Visalia's win, coupled with Lodi's 4-3 victory over Stockton, pulls the Oaks within one game of the pacesetting Ports. Lodi and Reno, a 2-1 winner over Fresno, both left the A's standing alone in fourth place.

Thursday night's hitters' jamboree included eight home runs and seven doubles. Visalia starter Jay Pettibone, 9-4, took the win, despite giving up 12 hits and seven runs.

Pettibone could afford the luxury, however — eight of the Oaks' first nine runs were unearned, as Modesto committed four errors and a host of other mistakes.

The A's Dwight Adams did smack a three-run homer in the fourth to close the gap to 9-6, but the Oaks' Scotti Madison closed the door in the sixth with his own three-run shot, his second of the game and 18th of the year.

Modesto took an early 2-1 lead on first-inning doubles by Don Hill and Wayne Rudolph, and Mickey Tettleton's homer in the second.

But Visalia exploded for five runs in the third — three on consecutive home runs by Ken Hrbek and Madison — before adding three in the fourth, two courtesy of Hrbek's second round-tripper.

As far as tonight, this would become a special night in the lives of the Visalia Oaks players, more than any other night during the season. From day one after breaking spring camp I sensed this would be a memorable season. The way it began with such a remarkable trip driving across country with Herbie would help set the stage as being my favorite summer of playing baseball. It was a trip I would never take again, and Visalia would serve as the sleepy little town where baseball was pure and innocent and every player's financial status encouraged him to get along with his teammates. We all pulled for each other the entire season, and tonight we, as a team, would be rewarded for that pureness of heart we still felt for the game of baseball.

We arrived at the park about the usual hour of 4:00 p.m. Being the home team, we would take batting practice first, as was customary, and the Lodi Dodgers, in town for a four-game series, would follow suit. Most of us were sitting in our hardback chairs, the only comfort we were afforded between our butts and the mixture of rough mortar and concrete that made up the locker room floor.

Not long into the pregame dress, Dick Phillips opened the door to his office, which never occurred until Skip was ready to walk out on the field. His room was one of secrecy, where we could hear conversations between Skip and the Minnesota Twins front office, as well as the occasional opening of a beer can before it found a home in Skip's liver. He was not one to call players into his office and discuss a problem. Looking back, I can remember only one time that I entered his office, and that was to discuss the Topps baseball card contract.

When the door suddenly opened, a hush came over the locker room as the players gazed at Skip. Some of us thought we were about to get a motivational speech from him before our opening game with the Lodi Dodgers. We had not heard a speech since the end of spring camp four months earlier, so it was about time for another "play hard and have fun" pep talk.

But all we heard was Dick Phillips saying, "Herbie, I need to see you!"

The locker room grew silent, and then a murmur of curiosity circled around the room: What had Herbie done? Was he in trouble? Why would Skip need to see him? After all there were some great-looking girls in Visalia who were a lot of fun, and many were trying to leave their simple Visalia existence by way of a good player on the Oaks. Herbie was one of the best players, if not the best player, on the Oaks, so that would be a good guess. Surely Herbie wasn't in trouble over, of all things, a girl? No, that wouldn't be the situation. No one on the team could have guessed the magnitude of Herbie's closed door meeting with Skip.

All eyes were on Skip's door, waiting for Herbie to venture out. When the door slowly opened, the tall and lanky Hrbek wandered out in what can only be described as a stupor. He was dazed and was fumbling to find the right words to say to his teammates.

As he began to talk, he looked like the star zombie in the movie *Night of the Living Dead*. He stuttered the memorable words, "I'm going to the big leagues!"

The entire locker room erupted with exhilaration, and we began to jump up and down and celebrate. We were slapping each other's hands, and every one of us was congratulating Herbie, who couldn't say another word. He just kept shaking his head in disbelief. His best friend on the team was Wolfy, and I swear I saw Wolfy crying like a little girl because he was so happy for Herbie.

It was the most exciting time in baseball that any of us on the Oaks had personally experienced. We were young in professional baseball, so the game had not jilted us yet. We were all convinced that Herbie's moving to the big leagues was truly due to our team effort. Our victories, our efforts, our belief in the team concept rewarded all of us by sending one of our own to the "field of dreams." There was no jealousy in the locker room that night, and every player had heartfelt happiness for Herbie's promotion. For the rest of the 1981 season we believed the team's effort sent Herbie to Yankee Stadium. Herbie was heading to Yankee Stadium, and we all felt we were traveling with him.

☎

Sad to say, it wasn't long, maybe a season or two away, before all of us or at least those of us still left in the game began to change our mind-sets about a teammate's promotion. The game hardened us,

Scotti and Herbie, Royal Stadium, 1987.

or more likely, some people in the game hurt our feelings. All of us soon learned what it felt like to be demoted or released. People lied to us, and "the business" of baseball became part of our lives. We would feel the pain of contract disputes, we would witness promotions of lesser players, and we would blame management for taking away the innocence we had enjoyed in baseball. The simplicity we felt when playing catch, once the essence of our lives, had fled to find younger, more talented players.

The purity of the game escaped our core, and baseball became a job, not a pastime. You became a victim of circumstances, and if you play this crazy ass game long enough, everyone becomes a victim of circumstances. At that future point, we sadly reacted to a promotion of a fellow teammate with the thought, *Why not me?* We coveted another man's success!

Yet that Sunday evening in Visalia, California, when Kent Hrbek was told he was going to Yankee Stadium, the game of baseball to all of us was still a game played by little boys. What a glorious day that was!

It probably would have been better for Herbie if he immediately left the park that night and flew to New York. He was an emotional wreck, and he couldn't think about anything other than his advancement.

Skip put him in the lineup and started him at first base one more time. Herbie struck out all four times against lefty Tom Klawitter of the Lodi Dodgers. I'm sure that Tom Klawitter thought after giving Herbie a pitching beat-down that he belonged in the big leagues too.

To this day Tom Klawitter probably tells the story of embarrassing Kent Hrbek on his last night in a Visalia Oaks uniform, and Herbie talks about hitting a home run in his first game in the Major Leagues. Both were probably equally important to each man's psychological well-being.

As if there was not already enough pressure on Herbie's last night in Single A ball, they delayed the game to introduce him to the sparse crowd as a newly promoted Minnesota Twin. The announcer brought him out to a standing ovation from both dugouts and the loyal Oaks fans: "Ladies and gentlemen, our Visalia Oaks first baseman, Kent Hrbek, has just been called up to the parent club, the Minnesota Twins. He will leave tomorrow for the big leagues, and tonight is his last night playing for the hometown Oaks."

That certainly put Herbie on the spot, but it instantly improved his social life. At least three groupies waited to say good-bye to him after the game, all hoping they might be able to catch a ride on Herbie's back to New York with a one-night stand.

After announcing Herbie's good fortune to the crowd, they brought him out to speak. Herbie was not one for public speaking, and looking back, I can't believe I actually thought he might leave us with a golden nugget of wisdom, motivating his teammates and loyal Oaks fans for a final time. Herbie took the microphone following what seemed to be a timeless reminder over the public address system of his California League stats. After clearing his throat, he said, "I have enjoyed it here, and right now we are in first place, so you guys win this shit!" End of speech and all the players looked at each other and laughed; that was the Herbie we loved and would terribly miss in the coming days.

I remained in the dugout for quite some time the night of Herbie's call-up. The Oaks clubhouse was adjacent to left field, so I could still hear the team celebrating Herbie's promotion, and the jubilation continued as long as Herbie stayed in the locker room. I would say my good-byes and well wishes to Herbie as the big first baseman set off for bigger fish to catch. Kent Hrbek traveled to Yankee Stadium alone the next day, leaving California on an early flight headed back East. I thought, *The New York media is in for quite a surprise!*

The next night, the first night my friend was gone, I lingered after the game in the Oaks dugout for an even longer time. The game against the Lodi Dodgers that night seemed to last an eternity because every inning someone was bringing the team news of Herbie's play-by-play exploits in Yankee Stadium. We would anxiously await the next runner to bring news of a game so far away, but so close to our hearts. I do remember Herbie's home run in the twelfth inning at Yankee Stadium sent those in the dugout into a new round of jubilation, even though we were losing to the Lodi Dodgers. It was as if the entire team was playing two games at once. I was exhausted as the team lived vicariously through our former teammate, nervously waiting in anticipation for Herbie's every bat.

After the game, sitting alone in deep thought, I couldn't help wondering what it would be like to get a hit against the Yankees, much less win the game with a home run in the twelfth inning, like the big first baseman had done. I was happy for my friend, yet I wondered whether I would ever get the chance to play in the big leagues.

My soul ached for an opportunity like Herbie's, and I hoped I would always be able to play baseball. I started to ponder the thoughts: *What if I never get the call? What if I never get a chance to play in the Major Leagues?*

After gathering up my gear, I walked to the Oaks locker room. The grounds crew had finished prepping the fields for the next day's game, and they were now turning the lights out at Recreation Park. The hour was late, and all the other players had dressed and left the clubhouse to go home. Only Oaks manager Dick Phillips remained in the locker room, and I could hear him through the door, talking to Minnesota about the game and everyone's individual performance. I could also hear him talk about Hrbek's home run in Yankee Stadium.

Kent Hrbek had hit his first home run in Yankee Stadium some two hours earlier, and I was sitting alone at my locker a long way off from my old friend. I contemplated the one thought that seemed to overwhelm my emotions: *Will I still love the game if I don't make it to the Major Leagues?*

I reminisced about the times my father and I played catch when I was a young boy. A smile came over my face as I looked across the locker room and spotted Herbie's empty locker.

I had my answer: I *knew* I would always love baseball!

Epilogue

The Detroit Tigers would beat the Texas Rangers 4–3 in a most uneventful game on July 6, 1985. The Tigers had just come off a World Championship victory the prior fall, and the team was still laced with many star players. Less noteworthy to the victory was the fact that a rookie named Scotti Madison had cracked the lineup. I would be placed in the lineup between Lance Parrish and Darrell Evans in the batting order, batting sixth, and I would not get a base hit that night. In fact, I never got a hit until my third season in the big leagues. It was October 2, 1987, exactly six years and thirty-nine days after Kent Hrbek laced his first single for the Minnesota Twins, when I got a Major League hit.

I endured much suffering before tasting the sweetness of success. Yet one memory gave me hope in the days of darkness. A moment in time, August 1981, encouraged me to never give up, to stay the course, and to be strong and courageous. Kent Hrbek's call to the Major Leagues should serve as a reminder to all of us: to everyone who ever played the game of baseball; to everyone who ever had a dream. Whatever your dream might look like, even as distant as your dream may seem to be, the truth be known, your dream is only just a phone call away.

Lawrence Journal World 10/3/

Madison finally hits as Royals trim Twins

KANSAS CITY, Mo. (AP) — Charles and Sandra Madison's neighbors didn't need to worry when they saw a light on Friday night long after bedtime for the rural Alabama couple.

They were probably too excited to go back to sleep after their son, Scotti, called to say he'd just gotten his first three major league hits — all doubles in Kansas City's 6-3 victory Friday night over the American League West champion Minnesota Twins.

It was a few minutes past 10 p.m. when Madison excused himself from a knot of reporters.

"I've got to call my folks," he said. "Collect. I'll be right back."

A catcher who spent seven years in the minor leagues, mostly in the Detroit Tigers' system, Madison was hitless in 23 major league at-bats when he doubled off Frank Viola in the second inning.

He wound up 3-4 and also scored on Danny Tartabull's fifth inning grand slam that gave the Royals a 5-2 lead and allowed Bret Saberhagen to gain the victory.

SABERHAGEN, 18-10, gave nine hits and had four strikeouts. Viola, who will start for the Twins next week in the American League playoffs, dipped to 17-10. Outfielder Kirby Puckett was 4-4 for the Twins.

Scotti Madison

night trying to get one more," he said.

Viola said he was not overly disappointed.

"I did my best out there. I just got myself in trouble," Viola said. "I let the bottom of the order hurt me. Scotti Madison killed me tonight. I got behind Tartabull. Good hitters hit mistake pitches and with a 3-1 count you can look for a certain pitch. He did, and he hit it."

Viola also said he's not concerned about his chances for the Cy Young Award.

"At this time of the season, we've done what we've done as a team. All the individual stuff doesn't matter right now," he said.

MINNESOTA   KANSAS CITY

the Twins.

Madison said his parents were both asleep in their home in Lillian, Ala., when he called.

"They said if I woke them up for any other reason they'd be upset," he said with a grin. "But when I told them I got to catch Sabes and I got my first hit in the major leagues, they said I can call any time of night for news like that. They're just good old country folk. They go to sleep at 9 o'clock every night. I don't think they went back to sleep, though. I bet they went downstairs and had a cup of coffee."

The three doubles almost paled compared with the thrill of catching the 1985 World Series most valuable player, Madison said.

"It was a thrill just catching Sabes. In 1985 I was home watching the World Series and I thought how great it would be to catch him in a game. Here I am catching him in his last game of the season against the division champs. Seven years in the minor leagues was worth it."

TARTABULL'S GRAND slam gave him 33 homers and 99 runs batted in this season.

"I've got 99 runs batted in now and I'll be out there tomorrow

MINNESOTA					KANSAS CITY				
	ab	r	h	bi		ab	r	h	bi
Gladden lf	4	0	0	0	Wilson cf	4	1	2	2
Gagne ss	3	2	1	0	Seitzer 3b	3	1	1	0
Puckett cf	4	1	4	0	Brett 1b	4	0	0	0
Hrbek 1b	3	0	1	2	Trtabll rf	4	1	1	4
Gaetti 3b	4	0	0	0	FWhite dh	4	0	1	0
Bush dh	4	0	0	0	BJacksn lf	4	0	0	0
Brnnsky rf	4	0	1	0	Madison c	4	1	3	0
Lmbrdz 2b	3	0	1	0	Pecota ss	2	1	0	0
Newmn 2b	0	0	0	0	RoJons 2b	4	1	0	0
Smlly ph	1	0	0	0					
Laudner c	3	0	1	0					
Nieto c	0	0	0	0					
Lrkn ph	1	0	0	0					
Totals	34	3	9	2	Totals	33	6	8	6

Minnesota	000 110 010—3
Kansas City	000 051 00x—6

Gagne reached on catcher's interference.
Game Winning RBI — Tartabull (21).
E—Madison, Brett, Gagne, Tartabull. DP—Kansas City 2. LOB—Minnesota 6, Kansas City 6. 2B—Puckett 2, Madison 3, Wilson. HR—Tartabull (33). SF—Hrbek.

	IP	H	R	ER	BB	SO
Minnesota						
Viola L,17-10	6	7	6	2	3	5
Berenguer	1	1	0	0	0	2
Reardon	1	0	0	0	0	1
Kansas City						
Saberhagen W,18-10	9	9	3	2	0	4

Umpires—Home, Garcia; First, Reed; Second, Merrill; Third, Hirschbeck. T—2:23. A—22,578.

Kent Hrbek and Scotti, Royal Stadium 1987.

About the Author

SCOTTI MADISON is a 1981 graduate of Vanderbilt University, who lettered in two sports there. He was quarterback on the football team and catcher on the baseball team. He was born and raised in Pensacola, Florida, attending J. M. Tate High School, where he played football under his legendary uncle Carl Madison, the winningest high school football coach in the state of Florida. After being selected All-Southeastern Conference three times and All-American his senior year, he began his professional baseball career with the Minnesota Twins organization. His Minor League travels started with the Twins and sent him to the Los Angeles Dodgers and then Detroit Tigers his first five seasons. His last five took him to the Major Leagues with the Detroit Tigers, Kansas City Royals, and Cincinnati Reds for brief stints. During his professional baseball career, starting in 1978, he sold insurance for Aflac and won every sales award with the company. He was the number one salesman out of 60,000 Aflac agents. After being the top salesman for seven years in a row, he was presented the Chairman Emeritus Award, the first of its kind at Aflac for distinguished sales achievement. He has two children whom he loves dearly, Tori, age twenty-three, and Trent, age twenty-two.

◆

To learn more about Scotti Madison
and his book *Just a Phone Call Away* or to contact him
about a speaking engagement, go to
www.scottimadison.com.

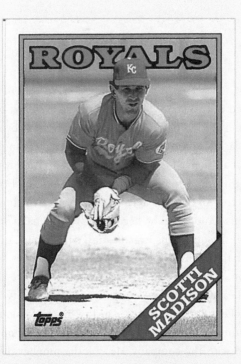

ROYALS

SCOTTI MADISON

Topps

SCOTTI MADISON ◆ C/1B

63T HT: 5'11" WT: 195 BATS: BOTH THROWS: RIGHT DRFT: TWINS #3 JUNE, 1980.
ACQ: FREE AGENT, 11-14-86 BORN: 9-12-59, PENSACOLA, FLA. HOME: NASHVILLE, TENN.

COMPLETE MAJOR & MINOR LEAGUE BATTING RECORD

YR CLUB	G	AB	R	H	2B	3B	HR	RBI	SB	SLG	BB	SO	AVG
80 ORLANDO	81	282	31	65	9	4	6	32	1	.355	46	39	.230
81 VISALIA	133	459	109	157	32	3	26	110	19	.595	91	53	.342
82 SAN ANTONIO	88	294	39	69	11	2	7	35	4	.357	54	27	.235
82 ALBUQUERQUE	11	36	5	8	1	0	0	2	0	.250	4	5	.222
83 SAN ANTONIO	80	259	54	79	11	4	11	57	5	.506	47	27	.305
83 ALBUQUERQUE	23	65	10	19	2	0	2	12	2	.415	13	6	.292
84 BIRMINGHAM	133	473	82	129	23	4	15	83	7	.433	94	63	.273
85 BIRMINGHAM	37	121	28	39	8	1	5	25	2	.529	35	12	.322
85 NASHVILLE	86	317	59	108	23	4	16	54	3	.590	43	45	.341
85 TIGERS	6	11	0	0	0	0	0	1	0	.000	2	0	.000
86 TIGERS	2	7	0	0	0	0	0	1	0	.000	0	3	.000
86 NASHVILLE	106	354	52	91	15	4	10	41	3	.407	51	49	.257
87 OMAHA	125	454	68	123	31	2	22	83	3	.493	60	50	.271
87 ROYALS	7	15	4	4	3	0	0	0	0	.467	1	5	.267
MIN. LEA. TOTALS	903	3114	537	887	166	28	120	534	49	.472	538	376	.285

GW-RBI (1987): 11   GW-RBI (CAREER): 67

** **

CPSIA information can be obtained at www.ICGtesting.com
Printed in the USA
LVOW011241121212

311327LV00001B/1/P